WORKBOOK

to accompany
the Second Edition of
DONALD M. AYERS'S

English
words

from Latin and
Greek elements

HELENA DETTMER

MARCIA LINDGREN

THE UNIVERSITY OF ARIZONA PRESS

Tucson & London

About the Authors

HELENA DETTMER is an Associate Professor in the Department of Classics at the University of Iowa. Before joining the staff there, she obtained a B.A. degree with honors in Classics at Indiana University and earned M.A. and Ph.D. degrees at the University of Michigan. Dettmer was a Mellon Fellow at Duke University for 1978–1979, and she was the recipient of the 1983 May Brodbeck Faculty Award at Iowa for her innovative research on the Latin poet Catullus.

MARCIA LINDGREN earned a baccalaureate degree with honors from Southern Connecticut State University. She went on to graduate study in Classics at the University of Iowa, where she received her M.A. and Ph.D. degrees. She has taught in the Department of Classics at Iowa and is currently an assistant to the Dean of the College of Liberal Arts.

NOTE

Words used in this text which the authors have reason to believe constitute trade names have been designated as such. However, neither the presence nor absence of such designation should be regarded as affecting the legal status of any trademark.

Fourth printing 1993

THE UNIVERSITY OF ARIZONA PRESS

ISBN 0-8165-0905-0

TABLE OF CONTENTS

Appendixes

PREFACE

This workbook began as a series of worksheets in vocabulary-building classes at the University of Iowa. It serves as a companion to the new edition of Donald M. Ayers's English Words from Latin and Greek Elements revised by Thomas D. Worthen. The workbook is designed to provide practice with Latin and Greek prefixes, bases, and suffixes introduced in the text and with English words derived from these elements.

The exercises require brief responses and take a variety of forms, including short answer, matching, multiple choice, word analysis, fill-in-the-blanks, and true-false. The bases introduced in the textbook determine the number and types of exercises in each lesson: while some elements, particularly Latin verbal bases, have many English derivatives, others have few. The variety of exercises is intended to give teachers choices in supplementing their instruction. It is expected that few will wish to assign every exercise in every lesson.

It should be noted that Part II of the workbook omits the scientific and medical bases introduced in Lessons XX-XXV. It was felt that the exercises in the textbook are more than adequate for these lessons, since in-depth study of scientific and medical terminology usually is reserved for a separate course.

Nearly every lesson in the workbook contains one or more exercises designed to provide further practice with elements learned in previous lessons. Major review sections occur periodically, and there is a comprehensive review at the end of Part I (Latin) and Part II (Greek). Latin review exercises also are included in Part II to allow students to prepare for a comprehensive final examination or simply to refresh their knowledge of Latin elements. So that students may practice independently, answers to the major and comprehensive reviews are given in Appendix B.

Completion of the exercises requires a knowledge of the Latin and Greek elements introduced in the textbook and the use of a standard college dictionary, such as Webster's New Collegiate Dictionary, The Random House College Dictionary, or The American Heritage Dictionary. On rare occasions words or etymologies are introduced that appear only in larger dictionaries.

The workbook should be used in combination with the exercises in the textbook. The exercises in the text present English words in sentences, while the workbook deals almost exclusively with words out of context. For this reason, the workbook can introduce a far greater number of words. Both experiences are important for students seeking to enrich their vocabularies.

Instructors are urged to adapt the workbook to their own needs. For example, a teacher could assign certain exercises and consider others optional, assign alternate items, use particular exercises as the basis for class discussion, with or without previous preparation, use the workbook for independent study, or develop an effective correspondence course using the workbook in conjunction with the textbook. The pages of the workbook are perforated so that students may hand in homework.

From experience we have found that the true-false and words of interest exercises provide an excellent basis for class discussion. But since these exercises often are the most challenging and time-consuming for students to do on their own, an instructor may wish to go over some or all of the material in class without demanding previous preparation. The Latin review exercises with topical themes (food, occupations, etc.) also may furnish possible subjects for class discussion. For example, the review exercise on clothing (page 156) could serve as a point of departure for considering other items of apparel with interesting etymologies. In addition, any course in Latin and Greek etymology provides ample opportunity to discuss various aspects of Greek and Roman history and culture. For instance, the numerical bases introduced in Part I, Lesson VI, invite a discussion of the names of the months. An instructor could explain Julius Caesar's reforms of the Roman calendar, and how the Romans had an eight-day work week without weekends to recuperate.

We wish to thank our many students at the University of Iowa, who over the past four years have allowed us to test a great variety of exercises and who have provided us with numerous suggestions and comments. Professor Edward Schmoll and his students at the University of Missouri used a final edition of the workbook and shared their observations. Russell Clarke and Billie Anderson, graduate students in Classics at Iowa, assisted with word-processing. Ms. Anderson also provided assistance with the final proofreading, corrections, and modifications. Another graduate student, Joseph Hughes, often acted as a sounding board for specific items and general ideas. We also wish to thank R. L. Cherry for his many suggestions, both editorial and pedagogical. The authors are indebted to the Department of Classics of the University of Iowa for its support of this project.

Helena Dettmer and Marcia Lindgren

INTRODUCTION

Indicate whether each statement is true or false by circling T or F.

T F 1. English is linguistically midway between the Germanic and Latin languages.

T F 2. There is no recorded evidence of a Proto-Indo-European language.

T F 3. The English language has acquired the words noodle, pretzel, and delicatessen from German.

T F 4. Modern Greek is the single surviving representative of the Hellenic branch of the Indo-European family.

T F 5. Such words as alchemy, algebra, and cipher have entered the English language by way of the Moorish and Arabic cultures.

T F 6. The Roman occupation of Britain is reflected in the suffix -cester, -chester (Worcester, Dorchester), which derives from the Latin word for "camp."

T F 7. Ironically, English has borrowed no words from the languages of native Americans.

T F 8. It is easy to determine whether a Latinate word in English derives directly from Latin or enters English through French.

T F 9. Most of the principal languages of Europe belong to the Indo-European family.

T F 10. Many Dutch words that have entered the English language are concerned with sailing and art.

T F 11. The Romance languages, the descendants of Latin, do not reflect the vastness of the empire Rome once held.

T F 12. Cognate languages derive from a common ancestor.

T F 13. The pronouns of Modern English bear little resemblance to those of Old English.

T F 14. The battle of Hastings in 1066 is an event of little consequence for the development of the English language.

T F 15. In Great Britain, the French spelling of some words (such as colour and humour) has been retained, while in America the spelling has reverted to Latin.

PART I

WORD ELEMENTS FROM LATIN

LESSON I

Using your dictionary as an authority, indicate whether each
statement is true or false by circling T or F.

T F   1. Paraphernalia once referred to property besides dowry
           that a bride brought to the home of her new husband.
T F   2. Good humored should be written as one word
           (goodhumored).
T F   3. The etymological meaning of amethyst is "remedy against
           drunkenness."
T F   4. "Antennae" is the only plural form of antenna
           acceptable in formal English.
T F   5. The word cayuse is used chiefly in the western part of
           the United States.
T F   6. The plural of moose is "mooses."
T F   7. The primary accent of chiropodist falls on the second
           syllable.
T F   8. Pub is a shortened form of "public house."
T F   9. The word gerrymander is a coinage that combines the
           name of a former governor of Massachusetts, Elbridge
           Gerry, with "salamander."
T F 10. Lexicographers apply the terms obsolete and archaic
           indiscriminately to refer to any word not in use since
           1775.
T F 11. The word galluses is used informally as a synonym for
           "suspenders."
T F 12. Kerb is the British spelling of the American "curb."
T F 13. Common and vulgar can mean the same thing.
T F 14. The red condiment used by Americans to anoint
           hamburgers and French fries may be spelled "catchup,"
           "catsup," or "ketchup."
T F 15. The past tense of the verb drag is "drug."

LESSON II

1. Circle the letter of the correct definition. Be sure that nouns are defined by nouns, verbs by verbs, and adjectives by adjectives.

    1. <u>verbose</u>: (A) wordy (B) talkativeness (C) to use too many words

    2. <u>fortitude</u>: (A) strong (B) strength (C) to strengthen

    3. <u>divest</u>: (A) stripped (B) deprivation (C) to strip or deprive of anything

    4. <u>affirmation</u>: (A) indicating assent (B) a positive statement (C) to state positively

    5. <u>artificial</u>: (A) produced by man (B) something produced by man (C) to contrive

    6. <u>tripartite</u>: (A) divided into three parts (B) division into three parts (C) to divide into three parts

    7. <u>refinement</u>: (A) cultivated (B) elegance (C) to make more elegant

    8. <u>alienation</u>: (A) foreign, strange (B) estrangement (C) to make hostile

    9. <u>fortify</u>: (A) strong (B) strength (C) to strengthen

   10. <u>confirm</u>: (A) firmly established (B) proof (C) to prove

   11. <u>finale</u>: (A) pertaining to or coming at the end (B) conclusion (C) to conclude

   12. <u>aggrandize</u>: (A) increased in size or intensity (B) magnification (C) to make great

   13. <u>particularity</u>: (A) specific (B) a special characteristic (C) to treat in detail

   14. <u>linear</u>: (A) arranged in a line (B) division into lines (C) to outline

   15. <u>nullify</u>: (A) invalid (B) nothingness (C) to invalidate

2. Words of Interest. Supply the appropriate word from the list
   below.

	Word	Etymological Meaning	Current Meaning
1.	_____	a burdening	grounds for complaint; resentment
2.	_____	rented land	land on which crops and livestock are raised
3.	_____	cross-dresser	someone who wears the clothes of the opposite sex
4.	_____	reduction to nothing	total destruction
5.	_____	oily flax	a floor covering
6.	_____	divided or even game	danger
7.	_____	disguise	grotesque imitation
8.	_____	soft and loud	keyboard instrument in which hammers strike metal strings
9.	_____	cloth made of flax	intimate clothing worn by women
10.	_____	that which is firm or fixed	the heavens
11.	_____	work of art	trickery; cleverness
12.	_____	excessively concerned with fine points	fussy
13.	_____	byword	maxim; pithy saying
14.	_____	to settle a payment	to supply with capital
15.	_____	substance with slight affinity to other materials	waxy substance used in candles, etc.

annihilation   firmament   paraffin
artifice   grandam   pianoforte
farm   grievance   proverb
finance   jeopardy   transvestite
finesse   lingerie   travesty
finicky   linoleum   trombone

3.   ART-; FIN-; FIRM-; FORT-; GRAND-; LINE-; NIHIL-; NUL(L)-;
VERB-; VEST-

Circle the bases in the following words and then match each
with the best definition.

___	1. artisan	A.	excessively large in scope
___	2. definitive	B.	pertaining to words
___	3. fine	C.	to furnish with power
___	4. infirmary	D.	decisive
___	5. fortress	E.	strong point
___	6. forte	F.	a stronghold
___	7. comfort	G.	ancestry
___	8. grandiose	H.	sum of money exacted as a penalty
___	9. delineate	I.	craftsman
___	10. lineage	J.	to void
___	11. nihilism	K.	to trace in outline
___	12. annul	L.	small hospital
___	13. verbal	M.	to give strength
___	14. invest	N.	a place for keeping ceremonial garments
___	15. vestry	O.	total rejection of traditional values

4. Indicate whether the following pairs are synonyms or antonyms by circling S or A.

```
S  A   1.  gravity      -    solemnity
S  A   2.  infinite     -    limited
S  A   3.  finery       -    adornment
S  A   4.  grandeur     -    magnificence
S  A   5.  aggravate    -    improve
S  A   6.  align        -    adjust
S  A   7.  infirmity    -    healthiness
S  A   8.  verbatim     -    literally
S  A   9.  partisan     -    biased
S  A  10.  alien        -    familiar
S  A  11.  affinity     -    kinship
S  A  12.  grievous     -    oppressive
S  A  13.  artful       -    contrived
S  A  14.  verbiage     -    wordiness
S  A  15.  indefinite   -    certain
```

5. __PART-__

Match each word with the best definition.

```
___  1.  repartee        A.  a trace; speck
___  2.  particle        B.  to have a share
___  3.  impart          C.  a package
___  4.  partake         D.  a separate room or chamber
___  5.  parcel          E.  a witty reply
___  6.  departure       F.  a natural complement
___  7.  counterpart     G.  the act of leaving
___  8.  participle      H.  a social gathering
___  9.  compartment     I.  a verbal adjective
___ 10.  party           J.  to bestow
```

LESSON III

1. Circle the prefixes and bases and then give the meaning of
   each element. (Bases from Lesson II are included.)

		PREFIX	BASE
1.	advent	_____	_____
2.	abjure	_____	_____
3.	deprecate	_____	_____
4.	affinity	_____	_____
5.	circumlocutory	_____	_____
6.	deduction	_____	_____
7.	contravene	_____	_____
8.	aggrandizement	_____	_____
9.	divest	_____	_____
10.	counterpart	_____	_____
11.	annulment	_____	_____
12.	collude	_____	_____
13.	departure	_____	_____
14.	abscess	_____	_____
15.	circumvent	_____	_____
16.	comfort	_____	_____
17.	abstruse	_____	_____
18.	antecedent	_____	_____
19.	confirm	_____	_____
20.	aggravation	_____	_____

2. Words of Interest. Supply the appropriate word from the list below.

	Word	Etymological Meaning	Current Meaning
1.	_____	to come to mind	a memento
2.	_____	that which the earth brings forth	fresh fruit and vegetables
3.	_____	belly-speaker	one who throws his voice
4.	_____	removal of meat	Mardi gras; festival
5.	_____	to lead out (a child)	to instruct
6.	_____	a wrong	damage; pain
7.	_____	thrust out of sight	difficult to understand
8.	_____	area over which an official speaks the law	authority to exercise control
9.	_____	one recently arrived	upstart
10.	_____	something about to happen	an undertaking involving risk
11.	_____	light (sleight) of hand	trickery; deception
12.	_____	a coming together	assembly of witches

abstruse	injury	levy
adventure	jurisdiction	parvenu
carnival	jurisprudence	produce
coven	leaven	souvenir
educate	legerdemain	ventriloquist

3. Indicate whether the following pairs are synonyms or antonyms
    by circling S or A.

```
S  A   1.  obloquy          -   abuse
S  A   2.  obtrusive        -   inconspicuous
S  A   3.  levity           -   gravity
S  A   4.  prevent          -   hinder
S  A   5.  alleviate        -   oppress
S  A   6.  ludicrous        -   comical
S  A   7.  deprecate        -   disapprove
S  A   8.  contravene       -   oppose
S  A   9.  adjust           -   arrange
S  A  10.  conventional     -   original
S  A  11.  intervene        -   meddle
S  A  12.  colloquial       -   formal
S  A  13.  irrelevant       -   pertinent
S  A  14.  unproductive     -   prolific
S  A  15.  imprecate        -   curse
```

4. <u>DUC-, DUCT-</u>

    Match each word with the best definition.*

```
____  1.  abduction           A.  subtraction
____  2.  conduct             B.  sexual enticement
____  3.  deduction           C.  something manufactured
____  4.  eduction            D.  kidnapping
____  5.  inducement          E.  installation into office
____  6.  induction           F.  generation of offspring
____  7.  introduction        G.  inference; elicitation
____  8.  product             H.  deportment; behavior
____  9.  reduction           I.  preface
____ 10.  reproduction        J.  incentive
____ 11.  seduction           K.  slander
____ 12.  traducement         L.  diminution
```

*The verbs that correspond to these nouns end in -duce or
 -duct: <u>abduce</u>, <u>abduct</u>, <u>conduct</u>, <u>deduce</u>, <u>deduct</u>, etc.

5. Indicate whether each statement is true or false by circling T
    or F.

T   F   1. A <u>somniloquist</u> is unlikely to find success in a career
            as a double agent.
T   F   2. The word <u>alibi</u> means that a person was "elsewhere" when
            the crime was committed.
T   F   3. The etymological meaning of <u>null</u> is "not any."
T   F   4. A <u>grievous</u> error is one of little consequence.
T   F   5. The noun <u>decedent</u> is roughly equivalent to the
            euphemistic expression "to pass away."
T   F   6. An <u>alienee</u> is a female extraterrestrial.
T   F   7. <u>Paraffin</u> derives its name from its relative lack of
            affinity to other materials.
T   F   8. "Fort-" in <u>fortnight</u> derives from the Latin base FORT-.
T   F   9. <u>Hoosegow</u>, slang for "jail," ultimately derives from the
            Latin base JUDIC-.
T   F 10. The etymology of <u>precarious</u> ("depending on prayer")
            suggests the uncertain relationship that the Romans had
            with their gods, whereby praying was "risky" business.

6. <u>JUR-</u>

    Match each word with the best definition.*

____ 1. abjure   A. to command solemnly
____ 2. adjure   B. to harm
____ 3. conjure   C. to recant; to renounce
____ 4. injure   D. to swear falsely under oath
____ 5. perjure   E. to summon by incantation

    *The nouns that correspond to these verbs end in -jury or
    -juration: <u>abjuration</u>, <u>adjuration</u>, etc.

7. CED-, CESS-

Match each word with the best definition.*

___	1. access	A.	superabundance
___	2. antecedent	B.	acknowledgment; subsidiary
___	3. concession		business
___	4. excess	C.	suspension of activities
___	5. intercession	D.	a continuous, orderly movement
___	6. precedent		of people or objects; parade
___	7. procession	E.	forebear
___	8. recess	F.	achievement
___	9. secession	G.	example; model
___	10. success	H.	formal withdrawal
		I.	approach
		J.	mediation

*With the exceptions of access and recess, the verbs that correspond to these nouns end in -ceed or -cede: accede, antecede, concede, etc.

8. LUD-, LUS-

Match each word with the best definition.*

___	1. allusion	A.	conspiracy
___	2. collusion	B.	evasion
___	3. delusion/illusion	C.	indirect reference
___	4. elusion	D.	introduction
___	5. prelusion (prelude)/	E.	self-deception; deception
	prolusion		

*The verbs that correspond to these nouns end in -lude: allude, collude, etc.; the adjectives end in -lusive or -lusory: allusive, collusive, delusive or delusory, etc.

9. **Review:** Indicate whether the following pairs are synonyms or antonyms by circling S or A.

S	A	1.	ad infinitum	-	forever
S	A	2.	judicious	-	sensible
S	A	3.	inalienable	-	transferable
S	A	4.	aggravate	-	worsen
S	A	5.	annihilate	-	nullify
S	A	6.	elevate	-	lower
S	A	7.	success	-	failure
S	A	8.	prejudiced	-	impartial
S	A	9.	educated	-	knowledgeable
S	A	10.	verbose	-	laconic
S	A	11.	reduction	-	increment
S	A	12.	interlocutory	-	provisional
S	A	13.	definitive	-	inconclusive
S	A	14.	adjure	-	exhort
S	A	15.	alignment	-	adjustment

10. **Review:** Match each word with the best definition.

___ 1.	infirm	A.	a share
___ 2.	fort	B.	invalidity
___ 3.	investiture	C.	contrivance
___ 4.	refined	D.	remorse
___ 5.	grief	E.	descent from a common ancestor
___ 6.	portion	F.	army post
___ 7.	particle	G.	"heavy with child": pregnant
___ 8.	enforce	H.	weak
___ 9.	grand	I.	positive; favoring
___10.	nullity	J.	the act of authorizing
___11.	alienate	K.	characterization
___12.	lineage	L.	to execute vigorously
___13.	artifice	M.	a person's strong point
___14.	affirmative	N.	purified; elegant
___15.	gravid	O.	to estrange
		P.	a very small portion
		Q.	lavish; sublime

LESSON IV

1. <u>GREG-</u>

Match each word with its <u>etymological</u> meaning.

___ 1.	gregarious	A.	a spiritual flock
___ 2.	egregious	B.	to keep from the flock
___ 3.	aggregate	C.	marked by a liking for the flock
___ 4.	congregation	D.	the sum of the flock
___ 5.	segregate	E.	standing out from the flock: conspicuously bad

2. <u>CRUC-; HAB-, AB-, (HIB-); PED-; PUNG-, PUNCT-; SACR-, (SECR-); SANCT-; SENT-, SENS-; TURB-; VI(A)-</u>

Match each word with the best definition.

___ 1.	crucial	A.	to make unnecessary
___ 2.	excruciating	B.	advantageous
___ 3.	prohibitive	C.	to profane
___ 4.	cohabit	D.	the pricking of conscience
___ 5.	exhibition	E.	hindrance
___ 6.	rehabilitate	F.	going on foot; commonplace
___ 7.	impediment	G.	to render fit again; to restore
___ 8.	expedient	H.	decisive
___ 9.	pedestrian	I.	supplies for a journey
___ 10.	punctuation	J.	to surrender anything for the sake of another
___ 11.	compunction	K.	to respond emotionally to an indignity
___ 12.	pungent		
___ 13.	desecrate	L.	public display
___ 14.	sacrifice	M.	biting; acrid
___ 15.	sanctimonious	N.	hypocritically devout
___ 16.	resent	O.	periods or commas, for example
___ 17.	sentiment	P.	cloudy; confused
___ 18.	turbid	Q.	to live together as husband and wife
___ 19.	viaticum	R.	agonizing
___ 20.	obviate	S.	a feeling colored by emotion
		T.	serving to prevent

17

3. Words of Interest. Supply the appropriate word from the list below.

	Word	Etymological Meaning	Current Meaning
1.	_____	off the beaten track	indirect; tricky
2.	_____	foot of a crane	genealogy
3.	_____	holy place	refuge
4.	_____	to mark out with dots	to delete
5.	_____	a gathering (stealing) of sacred things	profanation
6.	_____	to sail across	to travel about
7.	_____	on the dot	prompt
8.	_____	where three roads meet	insignificant
9.	_____	foot soldier	person earliest in a field of inquiry
10.	_____	a cross	perplexing difficulty
11.	_____	a turning	personal account of something
12.	_____	to free the foot	to facilitate
13.	_____	doubly holy	inviolable
14.	_____	a turning by a plow	a line of poetry
15.	_____	a small point	precise observance of forms

cruise	expunge	sacrilege
crusade	pedigree	sacrosanct
crux	pioneer	sanctum
devious	prose	trivial
dishabille	punctilio	verse
expedite	punctual	version

4. Indicate whether each statement is true or false by circling T or F.

T F   1. An <u>inhibited</u> person is unlikely to apply for a job as an <u>ecdysiast</u>.
T F   2. <u>Pedal</u> and its homophone <u>peddle</u> derive from the same Latin base.
T F   3. People who speak in a <u>circumlocutory</u> manner get right to the point.
T F   4. The basic meaning of <u>scent</u> is "perception or feeling through the olfactory organs."
T F   5. <u>Verse</u> and <u>prose</u> (> proversus) both belong to the VERT-VERS- family of words.
T F   6. The prefix in <u>dissent</u> has undergone assimilation.
T F   7. <u>Crucible</u> can refer to any severe, trying test.
T F   8. <u>SALT</u> is an acronym for the Strategic Arms Limitation Talks of the 1970's.
T F   9. The expression <u>sacred cow</u> owes its derivation to the ancient Roman practice of worshiping Juno, the "ox-eyed" goddess.
T F 10. In words like proportion, apportion, etc., the Latin base PART- appears as PORT-.

5. Indicate whether the following pairs are synonyms or antonyms by circling S or A.

S A   1. adversity   -   prosperity
S A   2. assent   -   disagree
S A   3. diverse   -   manifold
S A   4. obvious   -   abstruse
S A   5. habit   -   custom
S A   6. perturbable   -   unruffled
S A   7. sententious   -   pithy
S A   8. versed   -   skilled
S A   9. habitat   -   environment
S A 10. versatile   -   unadaptable
S A 11. execrable   -   detestable
S A 12. invertebrate -   weak
S A 13. impervious   -   penetrable
S A 14. adversary   -   foe
S A 15. sanction   -   approve

6. <u>VERT-, VERS-</u>

Match each word with the best definition.*

____ 1.	aversion	A.	a turning inward: preoccupation with oneself
____ 2.	advertence	B.	regression
____ 3.	animadversion	C.	dispute
____ 4.	conversion	D.	the reverse
____ 5.	controversy	E.	severe, unjust criticism
____ 6.	diversion	F.	the act of turning so as to present a different side
____ 7.	inversion	G.	the overturning of a government, for example
____ 8.	introversion	H.	distortion
____ 9.	obversion	I.	a turning of one's attention
____10.	perversion	J.	a turning away from: repugnance
____11.	reversion	K.	the act of embracing an idea or religious faith
____12.	subversion	L.	amusement

*The verbs that correspond to these nouns end in -vert: <u>avert</u>,
<u>advert</u>, <u>animadvert</u>, etc.

7. The French Connection. Supply the appropriate word from the
list below.

1. a regular customer _____

2. from head to foot _____

3. a literary postscript _____

4. to call attention to
a product _____

5. very moving _____

6. ailment; disorder _____

7. dissolution of a
marriage _____

8. state of disorder _____

9. travel by air or sea _____

10. worry; inconvenience _____

advertise   envoi   pied-à-terre
cap-a-pie   habitué   poignant
dishabille   malady   trouble
divorce   pedigree   voyage

8. Review: Supply the missing prefix or base.

1. seriousness   _ _ _ _ ity
2. weak; sickly   _ _ firm
3. word-for-word   _ _ _ _ atim
4. unfeeling   in _ _ _ _ itive
5. strength   _ _ _ _ itude
6. to end   _ _ _ ish
7. to prick   _ _ _ _ _ ure
8. to reduce to nothing an _ _ _ _ _ ate
9. a go-between   _ _ _ _ _ cessor
10. holy   _ _ _ _ ed
11. talkative   _ _ _ _ acious
12. limitless   _ _ finite
13. to clothe   v _ _ _
14. byword   _ _ _ verb
15. lightness   _ _ _ ity
16. cross-shaped   _ _ _ _ iform

21

17. by way of   v _ _

18. to lead away by force   _ _ duct

19. pertaining to the foot   _ _ _ al

20. to do wrong to   _ _ jure

9. **Review:** Circle the letter of the word that best fits the definition.

1. to escape:
   - (A) allude
   - (B) collude
   - (C) elude
   - (D) prelude

2. to force in:
   - (A) extrude
   - (B) intrude
   - (C) obtrude
   - (D) protrude

3. a decrease:
   - (A) induction
   - (B) production
   - (C) reduction
   - (D) seduction

4. to reject solemnly:
   - (A) abjure
   - (B) adjure
   - (C) conjure
   - (D) perjure

5. self-deceptive:
   - (A) allusive
   - (B) delusive
   - (C) elusive
   - (D) prelusive

6. to grant grudgingly:
   - (A) concede
   - (B) exceed
   - (C) proceed
   - (D) recede

7. to kidnap:
   - (A) abduct
   - (B) conduct
   - (C) deduct
   - (D) induct

8. economic slowdown: (A) accession
                                (B) cession
                                (C) intercession
                                (D) recession

9. to purify: (A) confine
                                (B) define
                                (C) fine
                                (D) refine

10. movingly expressive: (A) circumlocutory
                                (B) colloquial
                                (C) eloquent
                                (D) loquacious

11. to oppose: (A) contravene
                                (B) convene
                                (C) intervene
                                (D) supervene

12. alluring: (A) inductive
                                (B) productive
                                (C) reductive
                                (D) seductive

13. to elicit: (A) adduce
                                (B) educe
                                (C) reduce
                                (D) traduce

14. endowment: (A) circumvention
                                (B) invention
                                (C) prevention
                                (D) subvention

15. introductory: (A) delusory
                                (B) illusory
                                (C) ludicrous
                                (D) prelusory

16. dialogue: (A) colloquy
                                (B) elocution
                                (C) obloquy
                                (D) soliloquy

17. upstart: (A) avenue
                                (B) parvenu
                                (C) revenue
                                (D) venue

18. elaborate adornment:
   (A) affinity
   (B) finality
   (C) finery
   (D) infinity

19. to live in:
   (A) cohabit
   (B) habilitate
   (C) inhabit
   (D) rehabilitate

20. a dislike:
   (A) aversion
   (B) obversion
   (C) reversion
   (D) subversion

10. Review: The French Connection. Match each word with the base from which it derives.

___ 1. subdue   A. CED-, CESS-
___ 2. grief   B. DUC-, DUCT-
___ 3. travesty   C. FORT-
___ 4. avenue   D. GRAV-
___ 5. jury   E. JUR-, JUST-
___ 6. deceased   F. LEV-
___ 7. enforce   G. LINE-
___ 8. lingerie   H. PART-
___ 9. parcel   I. PUNG-, PUNCT-
___10. relieve   J. VEN-, VENT-
___11. appoint   K. VERB-
___12. verbiage   L. VEST-

LESSON V

1. Give the unassimilated forms of the prefixes in the following
    words.

    1. success   _____   10. correct   _____
    2. assent   _____   11. approve   _____
    3. impartial   _____   12. offer   _____
    4. collude   _____   13. aggregate   _____
    5. arrogant   _____   14. effort   _____
    6. sufficient   _____   15. differ   _____
    7. occurrence   _____   16. acquire   _____
    8. illuminate   _____   17. supply   _____
    9. affable   _____   18. irrevocable _____

2. GRAD-, GRESS-

    Match each word with the best definition.*

    ___ 1. aggression   A. return; reversion

    ___ 2. digression   B. exit

    ___ 3. egress or egression   C. sin; infringement

    ___ 4. ingress or ingression   D. forward movement

    ___ 5. progress or progression   E. entry

    ___ 6. regress or regression   F. hostility; offensive act

    ___ 7. transgression   G. excursion

    *The verbs that correspond to these nouns end in -gress:
    aggress, digress, etc. The adjectives end in -gressive:
    aggressive, digressive, etc.

3. Words of Interest.   Supply the appropriate word from the list below.

	Word	Etymological Meaning	Current Meaning
1.	_____	likely to see visions	impractical
2.	_____	something that enters into a mixture	component
3.	_____	a running	course of study
4.	_____	clear sight	intuitive insight
5.	_____	a list of words	words of a language
6.	_____	to admit to the next step	to receive a degree or diploma
7.	_____	looking all around	cautious
8.	_____	to look upon maliciously	to begrudge; to covet
9.	_____	foresighted	judicious
10.	_____	something weighed	a Mexican coin
11.	_____	bird-watching	favorable; propitious
12.	_____	a pausing to look back	interval of relief
13.	_____	word or phrase that fills out	an obscenity
14.	_____	place where medicine is weighed out	free clinic
15.	_____	runner	messenger

auspicious	distillery	prudent
circumspect	envy	respite
clairvoyance	expletive	specie
courier	graduate	spice
curriculum	ingredient	visionary
dispensary	peso	vocabulary

In the following two exercises, match each word with the best definition.

4. CLUD-, CLUS- *

      ____ 1. conclude   A. to prevent; to make impossible
      ____ 2. exclude   B. to finish
      ____ 3. include   C. to place in solitude; to isolate
      ____ 4. occlude   D. to shut out
      ____ 5. preclude   E. to bring cusps of upper and
      ____ 6. seclude   lower teeth into alignment
                                       F. to be made up of; to contain

   *The nouns that correspond to these verbs end in -clusion:
   conclusion, exclusion, etc. The adjectives end in -clusive:
   conclusive, exclusive, etc.

5. CLOS- *

      ____ 1. close   A. to surround
      ____ 2. disclose   B. to shut; to conclude
      ____ 3. enclose   C. to deprive of the right to
      ____ 4. foreclose   renew mortgaged property
                                       D. to reveal

   *The nouns that correspond to these verbs end in -closure:
   closure, disclosure, etc.

6. Supply the missing prefix or base.

      1. to oversee   _ _ _ _ _ vise

      2. forerunner   pre _ _ _ _ or

      3. hanging downward   _ _ _ _ ulous

      4. a calling   _ _ _ ation

      5. fullness   _ _ _ _ itude

      6. sight   _ _ _ ion

7. step by step   _ _ _ _ ual

8. to wave   _ _ _ ulate

9. payment   com _ _ _ _ ation

10. looking backward   _ _ _ _ _ spective

11. to look down on   _ _ spise

12. unrehearsed performance   impro _ _ _ ation

13. imminent   _ _ pending

14. to pay out   _ _ pend

15. incapable of being seen   in _ _ _ ible

7. Indicate whether the following pairs are synonyms or antonyms by circling S or A.

S	A	1.	deplete	-	fill
S	A	2.	cursory	-	hasty
S	A	3.	suspicious	-	questionable
S	A	4.	degrade	-	promote
S	A	5.	redundant	-	deficient
S	A	6.	speculate	-	conjecture
S	A	7.	implement	-	perform
S	A	8.	inspect	-	scrutinize
S	A	9.	inconclusive	-	final
S	A	10.	abundant	-	plentiful
S	A	11.	suspend	-	delay
S	A	12.	congress	-	convention
S	A	13.	special	-	ordinary
S	A	14.	vociferous	-	soft-spoken
S	A	15.	append	-	attach

8. <u>VOC-, VOK-</u>

    Match each word with the best definition.*

    ___ 1. advocate   A. to call together
    ___ 2. convoke   B. to call on for assistance;
    ___ 3. equivocate   to solicit
    ___ 4. evoke   C. to speak evasively
    ___ 5. invoke   D. to rescind
    ___ 6. provoke   E. to call forth
    ___ 7. revoke   F. to support verbally
                               G. to incite

    *The nouns that correspond to these verbs end in -vocation:
    <u>advocation</u>, <u>convocation</u>, etc.

9. Indicate whether each statement is true or false by circling T
    or F.

    T F 1. "To run to help" is the etymological meaning of <u>succor</u>.
    T F 2. A <u>digressive</u> style is characteristic of concise
              writing.
    T F 3. The etymological meaning of <u>preposterous</u> is "having the
              hindside first."
    T F 4. The life of a person living in a <u>cloister</u> is replete
              with social engagements.
    T F 5. Etymologically, a <u>pansy</u> is a "pensive"-looking flower.
    T F 6. An <u>egregious</u> error is one seldom detected.
    T F 7. <u>Curse</u> derives from the Latin base CUR(R)-, CURS-.
    T F 8. A permit of entry from one country into another is
              called a <u>visa</u>.
    T F 9. <u>Poison</u>, like <u>poise</u>, belongs to the PEND-, PENS- family
              of words.
    T F 10. Etymologically, a <u>millipede</u> is a "thousand-footer."

10. The French Connection. Supply the appropriate word from the list below.

1. to recommend   _____

2. a step or stage in a course or process   _____

3. pirate   _____

4. small room for storage   _____

5. to appraise (a situation)   _____

6. a strong liking   _____

7. to declare openly   _____

8. a very small amount   _____

9. grace; special ability   _____

10. to refill   _____

11. pun   _____

12. to result; to contribute   _____

13. a style of enamelware   _____

14. malice   _____

15. unrefined   _____

accomplishments	coarse	redound
advise	corsair	replenish
avow	degree	soupçon
cloisonné	equivoque	spite
closet	penchant	survey

11. **Review:** Circle the prefixes and bases and then match each word with the best definition.

____ 1. excursion

____ 2. invidious

____ 3. proverbial

____ 4. traverse

____ 5. interlinear

____ 6. reproduce

____ 7. congregate

____ 8. revenue

____ 9. perturbed

____ 10. secede

____ 11. introvert

____ 12. aggrieve

____ 13. presentiment

____ 14. interlocutor

____ 15. compunction

A. a feeling about the future

B. moving backward

C. remorse

D. upset; alarmed

E. a shy person

F. a brief trip

G. inserted between lines

H. to distress

I. to withdraw formally

J. to assemble

K. distorted

L. a person who takes part in a dialogue

M. tending to cause resentment

N. characteristic of a short, popular saying

O. income

P. to pass through

Q. to bring forth again

12. **Review:** Circle the letter of the word in each group that does not mean the same as the other two.

1. (A) appendix
    (B) compendium
    (C) conspectus

2. (A) advert
    (B) allude
    (C) espy

3. (A) dispense
    (B) apportion
    (C) expedite

4. (A) verbose
    (B) verbal
    (C) redundant

5. (A) evident
    (B) perspicacious
    (C) conspicuous

6. (A) obloquy
    (B) colloquy
    (C) conversation

7. (A) educible
    (B) breviloquent
    (C) compendious

8. (A) completion
    (B) close
    (C) subvention

9. (A) pedigree
    (B) alignment
    (C) ancestry

10. (A) occurrence
    (B) event
    (C) coven

11. (A) precursor
    (B) courier
    (C) antecedent

12. (A) obviate
    (B) prevent
    (C) suspend

13. (A) definitive
    (B) recurrent
    (C) conclusive

14. (A) annul
    (B) revoke
    (C) execrate

15. (A) special
    (B) particular
    (C) prosaic

16. (A) vouch
    (B) vilipend
    (C) despise

LESSON VI

1. Match each word with the best definition.

___ 1.	bipartite	A.	an introductory book
___ 2.	quincunx	B.	northern
___ 3.	primer	C.	college administrator
___ 4.	dub	D.	pit where stone is excavated
___ 5.	quarry	E.	having two parts
___ 6.	duplicity	F.	a three-legged stand
___ 7.	trivet	G.	to furnish with a new sound track
___ 8.	septentrional	H.	framework for growing vines
___ 9.	trellis	I.	deceit
___10.	dean	J.	arrangement of five objects

2. Identify the numerical base(s) in each of the following words and then give the meanings of the bases.

1. century _____

2. combine _____

3. decimate _____

4. deuce _____

5. mill _____

6. octave _____

7. prince _____

8. quarter _____

9. semiannual _____

10. squadron _____

11. trivial _____

12. unit _____

Part I, Lesson VI

3. Words of Interest. Supply the appropriate word from the list below.

	Word	Etymological Meaning	Current Meaning
1.	_____	nine each	devotion lasting nine days
2.	_____	a thousand paces	unit of distance equaling 5280 feet
3.	_____	fifth essence	the most typical representative
4.	_____	a foot and a half long	very long (used of words)
5.	_____	seventh month of early Roman calendar	ninth month of current calendar
6.	_____	a turning as one	cosmos
7.	_____	the ninth hour	midday
8.	_____	period of 40 days	isolation imposed to stop the spread of disease
9.	_____	the sixth hour	an afternoon nap
10.	_____	a single pearl	a bulb vegetable
11.	_____	two scale pans	poise; equilibrium
12.	_____	one of a kind	single; incomparable
13.	_____	three stakes (instrument of torture)	toil; suffering
14.	_____	period of six months	half of an academic year
15.	_____	of two minds	wavering

34

balance	novena	sesquipedalian
centurion	onion	siesta
dubious	quarantine	trammel
July	quintessence	travail
mile	semester	unique
noon	September	universe

4. **Review:** Match each prefix with the best definition.

___	1. ad-	A.	under; secretly
___	2. circum-	B.	apart; in different directions; not
___	3. dis-	C.	around
___	4. extra-	D.	back; again
___	5. per-	E.	after
___	6. re-	F.	outside; beyond
___	7. sub-	G.	to; toward
		H.	through; wrongly; completely
		I.	above; over
		J.	out; from

5. **Review:** Indicate whether each statement is true or false by circling T or F.

T F 1. Informally, "heads" and "tails" refer to the obverse and reverse sides of a coin.

T F 2. The Romans invented the punishment decimation to discourage mutiny in the ranks of the army.

T F 3. An alienist deals with persons exhibiting aberrant behavior.

T F 4. The words compliment and complement derive from different Latin bases.

T F 5. To speak vociferously is to speak softly.

T F 6. Lingerie once referred to linen goods in general.

T F 7. Pedestrian has come to mean "commonplace" because formerly those who walked were persons of low social status.

T F 8. The etymology of travel is "to labor."

T F 9. Etymologically, biscuit and zwieback mean the same thing.

T F 10. In English words, when the prefix ex- precedes a base beginning with "s," the "s" drops out (for example, execrate, expect).

6. **Review:** Use a check to indicate which of the following prefixes can act as intensifiers. (Intensifying prefixes have the force of "very," "completely," "thoroughly," "exceedingly," "vigorously," etc.)

    ____ 1. ad-
    ____ 2. con-
    ____ 3. de-
    ____ 4. ex-
    ____ 5. inter-

    ____ 6. ob-
    ____ 7. per-
    ____ 8. pre-
    ____ 9. sub-
    ____10. ultra-

7. **Review:** Use a check to indicate which of the following prefixes can mean "not."

    ____ 1. ab-
    ____ 2. circum-
    ____ 3. dis-

    ____ 4. in-
    ____ 5. non-
    ____ 6. post-

8. **Review:** Circle the letter of the word that best fits the definition.

    1. to call upon:

        (A) convoke
        (B) invoke
        (C) provoke
        (D) revoke

    2. thoughtful:

        (A) compendious
        (B) expensive
        (C) pendent
        (D) pensive

    3. to bring on oneself:

        (A) concur
        (B) incur
        (C) occur
        (D) recur

    4. ambiguous:

        (A) equivocal
        (B) provocative
        (C) vocalic
        (D) vociferous

5. to corrupt:
    (A) avert
    (B) divert
    (C) pervert
    (D) revert

6. an overstepping of bounds:
    (A) aggression
    (B) digression
    (C) regression
    (D) transgression

7. to shut out:
    (A) conclude
    (B) exclude
    (C) include
    (D) preclude

8. hobby:
    (A) avocation
    (B) convocation
    (C) equivocation
    (D) vocation

9. to empty:
    (A) complete
    (B) deplete
    (C) implement
    (D) replete

10. pastime:
    (A) diversion
    (B) eversion
    (C) inversion
    (D) subversion

11. to separate:
    (A) aggregate
    (B) congregate
    (C) desegregate
    (D) segregate

12. subtraction:
    (A) adduction
    (B) deduction
    (C) production
    (D) seduction

13. evasive:
    (A) circumlocutory
    (B) colloquial
    (C) eloquent
    (D) loquacious

14. source of protection:
    (A) concourse
    (B) course
    (C) discourse
    (D) recourse

15. to add:

(A) append
(B) expend
(C) impend
(D) suspend

16. secret agreement:

(A) collusion
(B) delusion
(C) elusion
(D) prolusion

17. to swear falsely
     under oath:

(A) abjure
(B) adjure
(C) conjure
(D) perjure

18. beyond the proper limit:

(A) concessive
(B) excessive
(C) recessive
(D) successive

19. to occur in
     consequence of:

(A) contravene
(B) convene
(C) intervene
(D) supervene

20. to disagree:

(A) assent
(B) dissent
(C) present
(D) resent

LESSON VII

1. Try to supply the appropriate word from the bases introduced
    in Lesson VII before referring to the list of possible choices
    at the end of the exercise.

    1. Tumors generally are classified as either _____
        or _____. The one is "kindly," the other fatal.

    2. A person "without care" is _____.

    3. A person who can write or speak many languages is
        _____.

    4. The adjective _____ means "without life" or
        "lifeless."

    5. The adjective _____ etymologically means "to be
        of one mind."

    6. A person wishing others well or good might be described as
        _____; a person wishing others evil, on the
        other hand, might be described as _____.

    7. The noun _____ etymologically means "the turning
        of a year."

    8. A person authorized to act for another is called a
        _____.

    9. Plants that live from year to year are called
        _____; plants that live for one year only are
        called _____.

    10. The adjective _____ etymologically means
        possessing "a noble (great) spirit."

    anniversary   inanimate   multilingual
    annuals   magnanimous   perennials
    annuities   malevolent   proxy
    benevolent   malignant   secure
    benign   malingerer   unanimous

39

2. <u>PLIC-, PLEX-, [PLY-]</u>

    Supply the appropriate word from the list below.

    1. to answer _____

    2. easily bent; flexible _____

    3. deception _____

    4. to make many or manifold _____

    5. a fold in clothing _____

    6. a set of three identical
        copies, "in _____" _____

    7. partner in crime _____

    8. the appearance and color of
        a person's skin, esp. the face _____

    9. to puzzle; to bewilder _____

    10. incapable of being explained _____

    11. to express indirectly _____

    12. a person who hires someone
        for wages _____

    13. to use selfishly; to take
        advantage of _____

    14. a copy; reproduction _____

    15. tangled; involved _____

accomplice	exploit	pleat
complex	imply	pliable
complexion	inexplicable	replica
duplicity	multiply	reply
employer	perplex	triplicate

Part I, Lesson VII

3. ANIM-; BENE-, BON-; CANT-, (CENT-); CUR-; EQU-, (IQU-); MAGN-;
MAL(E)-; MULT-

Match each word with the best definition.

___ 1.	animate	A.	to stress; to emphasize
___ 2.	animalcule	B.	"big shot"
___ 3.	beneficial	C.	sufficient
___ 4.	embellish	D.	an amoeba, for example
___ 5.	accentuate	E.	a job requiring little or no work
___ 6.	cant	F.	spiteful
___ 7.	sinecure	G.	to supervise an examination
___ 8.	accuracy	H.	advantageous
___ 9.	proctor (v.)	I.	an object causing attraction
___10.	adequate	J.	bombastic speech
___11.	equilibrium	K.	contraction of can not
___12.	magnate	L.	to enhance with ornamental details
___13.	magniloquence	M.	exactness
___14.	malicious	N.	balance
___15.	multifarious	O.	to enliven
		P.	having great variety
		Q.	jargon

4. Indicate whether each statement is true or false by circling T or F.

T F 1. The canary gets its name from the fact that it is a melodious songster.

T F 2. Magnum, as in "a magnum of champagne," derives from the Latin base MAGN-.

T F 3. The etymological meaning of incentive is "that which sets the tune," and hence incites to action.

T F 4. Duel ultimately derives from the Latin base BENE-, BON-.

T F 5. A bon mot is a particularly inappropriate word or expression.

T F 6. The magnolia derives its name from its large flowers.

T F 7. If a person is disenchanted, "the spell has worn off."

T F 8. Bonanza has a nautical derivation; originally the word meant "calm sea."

T F 9. The etymological meaning of debonair is "of good lineage."

T F 10. Bonbon and embonpoint both belong to the BON- family of words.

41

5. <u>FER-</u>

    Match each word with the best definition.

    _____ 1. circumference   A. a meeting for consultation
    _____ 2. conference   B. absence of interest
    _____ 3. deference   C. the favoring of one over another
    _____ 4. difference   D. perimeter
    _____ 5. indifference   E. a mention; footnote
    _____ 6. inference   F. logical conclusion from evidence
    _____ 7. preference   G. removal from one place to another
    _____ 8. reference   H. submission to opinion of another
    _____ 9. sufferance   I. disagreement
    _____ 10. transference   J. capacity to endure hardship

6. <u>LAT-</u>

    Match each word with the best definition.*

    _____ 1. collate   A. to fill with joy
    _____ 2. correlate   B. to carry over into another
    _____ 3. elate   language
    _____ 4. relate   C. to bring into mutual relation
    _____ 5. translate   D. to assemble pages of a document
                                          in their proper order
                                      E. to tell

    *The nouns that correspond to these verbs end in -lation;
    <u>collation</u>, <u>correlation</u>, etc.

7. Circle the letter of the correct word.

    1. A synonym for <u>retraction</u> that means "a singing back" is:
        (A) chanson (B) dirge (C) recantation

    2. A substance that brings or yields a fragrant odor is
        described as: (A) pungent (B) odoriferous
        (C) malodorous

    3. A person who usually looks on the bright side is a(n):
        (A) optimist (B) opportunist (C) beneficiary

4. A synonym for genuine that in Latin means "in good faith" is: (A) de facto (B) bona fide (C) ipsissima verba

5. An object of art whose value derives from its rarity or unusualness is called a: (A) sui generis (B) rara avis (C) curio

6. A synonym for composure that means "evenness of mind" is: (A) equanimity (B) equivocation (C) pusillanimity

7. A word describing a history of events in successive years is: (A) narrative (B) annals (C) excerpts

8. Another word for rooster that means "clear singer" is: (A) capon (B) cock (C) chanticleer

8. **Review**: Form the antonym of each word by substituting another prefix. Remember assimilation.

1. antebellum   _____ bellum

2. repletion   _____ pletion

3. dissent   _____ sent

4. explicit   _____ plicit

5. progress   _____ gress

6. consecrate   _____ secrate

7. recede   _____ ceed

8. divest   _____ vest

9. introverted   _____ verted

10. inhibit   _____ hibit

9. **Review:** The following words have entered English through Italian or Spanish. From the list below supply the base from which each derives.

<u>Italian</u>

1. punctilio _____

2. magnifico _____

3. vista _____

4. malaria _____

5. belladonna _____

6. fortissimo _____

7. finale _____

8. piedmont _____

9. grandioso _____

10. pococurante _____

11. squadron _____

12. canto _____

13. duce _____

14. replica _____

<u>Spanish</u>

1. corral _____

2. siesta _____

3. peon _____

4. bonanza _____

5. crusade _____

6. doubloon _____

7. peso _____

8. grandee _____

BENE-, BON-
CANT-, (CENT-)
CRUC-
CUR-
CUR(R)-, CURS-
DU-
DUC-, DUCT-

FIN-
FORT-
GRAND-
MAGN-
MAL(E)-
PED-
PEND-, PENS-

PLIC-, PLEX-
PUNG-, PUNCT-
QUADR(U)-
SEXT-
VID-, VIS-

REVIEW OF LESSONS II-VII

1. Give the unassimilated forms of the prefixes in the following words.

    1. annihilate   _____   6. imprecation   _____
    2. succor   _____   7. aggrandizement   _____
    3. compunction   _____   8. illusion   _____
    4. effort   _____   9. occlude   _____
    5. different   _____   10. suppliant   _____

2. Supply the appropriate prefix. Remember assimilation.

    1. to look down on   _____ spise

    2. to keep from the flock;
        to isolate   _____ gregate

    3. to lead away; to kidnap   _____ duct

    4. a going forward   _____ gress

    5. one who comes before   _____ cedent

    6. afterword   _____ script

    7. turned outward (outside)   _____ verted

    8. between the lines   _____ linear

    9. a coming to; arrival   _____ vent

    10. to turn a marriage
        contract asunder   _____ vorce

    11. looking backward   _____ spective

    12. a speaking together;
        conference   _____ loquy

    13. turned inward (within)   _____ verted

    14. an overstepping of bounds   _____ gression

15. allowing passage through   _____ vious

16. to oversee   _____ vise

17. to move back; to withdraw   _____ cede

18. a playing before   _____ lude or _____ lusion

19. to come upon; to discover   _____ vent

20. looking all around   _____ spect

3. Supply the missing base.

1. the best   _ _ _ _ _ um

2. serious   _ _ _ _ e

3. feeling   _ _ _ _ ation

4. hanging   _ _ _ _ ent

5. fullness   _ _ _ _ ty

6. lively   _ _ _ _ ated

7. a spell   in _ _ _ _ ation

8. unequalness   in _ _ _ ity

9. the end   _ _ _ is

10. period of 100 years   _ _ _ _ ennial

11. first   _ _ _ _ ary

12. speech spoken alone   soli _ _ _ _ y

13. oneness   _ _ ity

14. to wrong   in _ _ _ e

15. every two years   bi _ _ _ _ al

16. a calling   _ _ _ ation

17. to estrange   _ _ _ _ _ ate

18. twosome   _ _ o

19. evildoer   _ _ _ _ factor

20. to take part   _ _ _ _ icipate

21. wordiness   _ _ _ _ osity

22. the many   _ _ _ _ itude

23. person on foot   _ _ _ estrian

24. holiness   _ _ _ _ _ ity

25. greatness in size   _ _ _ _ itude

4. Match each word with the best description.

___ 1. pliable   A. to live from season to season
___ 2. gravamen   B. composed; dignified
___ 3. turbulent   C. tempestuous
___ 4. ability   D. flexible
___ 5. bonus   E. asymmetric
___ 6. poised   F. to declare; to utter
___ 7. voice   G. talent
___ 8. sensational H. exciting; stimulating
___ 9. disproportionate I. reward
___10. perennate   J. weightiest part of an accusation

5. Identify the numerical base in each of the following words.

1. binoculars   _____

2. duplicity   _____

3. mile   _____

4. October   _____

5. primrose   _____

6.   quarterback   _____

7.   quintessence   _____

8.   siesta   _____

9.   sesquipedality _____

10. trivet   _____

6. The words in the following exercise derive from Latin prefixes. Identify the prefix(es) and then give the current meaning of each word.

1. antics   _____

2. arrears   _____

3. contrary   _____

4. extraneous   _____

5. internal   _____

6. posthumous   _____

7. supernal   _____

8. ulterior   _____

7. Indicate whether the following pairs are synonyms or antonyms by circling S or A.

```
S  A   1.  excruciating   -    agonizing
S  A   2.  abstruse       -    evident
S  A   3.  infirm         -    invertebrate
```

S A   4. perturbable   -   serene
S A   5. circumvent   -   bypass
S A   6. replenish   -   empty
S A   7. revenant   -   ghost
S A   8. deprecate   -   approve
S A   9. traduce   -   malign
S A 10. curious   -   meddlesome
S A 11. fertile   -   unproductive
S A 12. provenance   -   origin
S A 13. inundate   -   flood
S A 14. relieve   -   oppress
S A 15. adjudge   -   decree
S A 16. inhabit   -   dwell
S A 17. pedigree   -   lineage
S A 18. proviso   -   stipulation
S A 19. expunge   -   insert
S A 20. induction   -   initiation

8. Words with Religious Associations. Match each word with the base from which it derives.

___ 1.	vow	A.	BENE-, BON-
___ 2.	saint	B.	CANT-, (CENT-), [CHANT-]
___ 3.	convent	C.	CED-, CESS-
___ 4.	habit	D.	CLUD-, CLUS-, [CLOS-]
___ 5.	crusade	E.	CRUC-
___ 6.	vestment	F.	CUR-
___ 7.	novena	G.	DECI(M)-
___ 8.	auspices	H.	HAB-, AB-, (HIB-)
___ 9.	Sistine	I.	NOVEM-
___10.	cloister	J.	PEND-, PENS-
___11.	vision	K.	PLE-, PLET-, PLEN-
___12.	dispensation	L.	PRIM-
___13.	curate	M.	SACR-, (SECR-)
___14.	processional	N.	SANCT-
___15.	benison	O.	SEXT-
___16.	dean	P.	SPEC-, (SPIC-), SPECT-
___17.	prioress	Q.	VEN-, VENT-
___18.	sacrament	R.	VEST-
___19.	chant	S.	VID-, VIS-
___20.	plenary (indulgence)	T.	VOC-, VOK-

9. **Review:** Choose the correct answer by circling A or B.

    1. main: (A) principal   (B) principle
    2. prudent: (A) judicial   (B) judicious
    3. hostile: (A) adverse   (B) averse
    4. stinging: (A) punctilious   (B) pungent
    5. wickedness: (A) inequity   (B) iniquity
    6. passport: (A) vista   (B) visa
    7. clear: (A) perspicacious   (B) perspicuous
    8. jealousy: (A) envoy   (B) envy
    9. thoughtful: (A) pensile   (B) pensive
   10. conclusive: (A) definite   (B) definitive
   11. foible: (A) infirmity   (B) infirmary
   12. dangerous: (A) precarious   (B) precatory
   13. money in coin: (A) specie   (B) species
   14. deceit: (A) duplication   (B) duplicity
   15. ghost: (A) spectre   (B) spectrum
   16. a yielding: (A) cession   (B) session
   17. fondness: (A) penchant   (B) pendant
   18. lewd: (A) sensual   (B) sensuous
   19. to escape: (A) allude   (B) elude
   20. savage: (A) primeval   (B) primitive

LESSON VIII

1. Indicate whether the following pairs are synonyms or antonyms by circling S or A.

    S A   1. temporary   - transient
    S A   2. corporeal   - spiritual
    S A   3. simulate   - counterfeit
    S A   4. tense   - strained
    S A   5. dissembler   - hypocrite
    S A   6. aquatic   - terrestrial
    S A   7. omnivorous   - finicky
    S A   8. extemporaneous   - improvised
    S A   9. corpulent   - slender
    S A 10. recto   - verso
    S A 11. obtain   - procure
    S A 12. tenuous   - substantial
    S A 13. impertinent   - rude
    S A 14. direct   - roundabout
    S A 15. retinue   - entourage

2. CORPOR-, CORP(US)-; REG-, (RIG-), RECT-; SIMIL-, SIMUL-; TEMPER-, TEMPOR-

    Match each word with the best definition.

    ___ 1. corpus   A. worldly
    ___ 2. incorporate   B. to disembody
    ___ 3. regular   C. an infectious viral disease
    ___ 4. erect   D. upright in position
    ___ 5. insurrection   E. to combine into one body
    ___ 6. directive   F. customary
    ___ 7. assemble   G. occurring at the same time
    ___ 8. simultaneous   H. a large collection of writings
    ___ 9. temporal   I. outburst of anger
    ___ 10. distemper   J. to bring together
                           K. rebellion
                           L. an order

Part I, Lesson VIII

3. TEN-, (TIN-), TENT-

Match each word with the best definition.*

___ 1. abstention   A. a holding in custody
___ 2. continence   B. food; nourishment
___ 3. detention   C. self-restraint; moderation
___ 4. entertainment   D. relevance
___ 5. maintenance   E. a vote neither for nor against
___ 6. pertinence   F. amusement; hospitality
___ 7. retention   G. lit. the state of holding in
___ 8. sustenance   the hand: means of support
                         H. memory

*The verbs that correspond to these nouns end in -tain:
abstain, contain, etc.

4. Circle the letter of the correct meaning of the underscored
    word.

    1. extenuating circumstances: (A) damning
                                  (B) embarrassing
                                  (C) providing an excuse

    2. resolved to temporize: (A) to postpone a decision
                                  (B) to dine on tempura
                                  (C) to make more even-
                                      tempered

    3. an Agatha Christie   (A) best seller
       omnibus: (B) a book of reprinted works
                                  (C) murder mystery

    4. corporal punishment: (A) capital
                                  (B) bodily
                                  (C) agonizing

    5. a tenable thesis: (A) consisting of ten parts
                                  (B) unsupportable
                                  (C) logical

    6. a musical ensemble: (A) group
                                  (B) composition
                                  (C) interlude

52

7. a scheduled <u>simulcast</u>:
    - (A) television documentary
    - (B) coverage of several athletic events in the same program
    - (C) a program broadcast at the same time on radio and TV

8. <u>aqueducts</u> built by the Romans:
    - (A) conduits for carrying water great distances
    - (B) temples
    - (C) water clocks

9. an assembled <u>corps</u>:
    - (A) unclaimed dead bodies
    - (B) a military body
    - (C) the complete and un-abridged works of an author

10. <u>contemporary</u> poetry:
    - (A) of the present time
    - (B) short-lived
    - (C) abstruse

5. Indicate whether each statement is true or false by circling T or F.

T F   1. The constellation <u>Aquarius</u> is the "water carrier."
T F   2. <u>Omnipresent</u> and <u>ubiquitous</u> are synonyms.
T F   3. A <u>contentious</u> person is congenial and easygoing.
T F   4. <u>Bus</u> is a shortened form of the Latin "omnibus."
T F   5. A <u>pastor</u> is the "shepherd" of a spiritual flock, a congregation.
T F   6. <u>Aqua vitae</u> ("the water of life") refers to strong liquor.
T F   7. <u>Charisma</u> ultimately derives from the Latin base CANT-.
T F   8. The prefix ad- has been assimilated in the word <u>aversion</u>.
T F   9. <u>Attenuate</u> and <u>extenuate</u> are opposite in meaning.
T F 10. -PLY is the French form of the Latin base PLIC-.
T F 11. <u>Resemblance</u> and <u>similarity</u> mean the same thing.
T F 12. A person who <u>abjures</u> physical exercise "swears by" (i.e., heartily recommends) it.
T F 13. The verb <u>expunge</u> derives from the Latin prefix ex- + SPONG- + the suffix -e.
T F 14. A <u>centurion</u> is a person celebrating a 100th birthday.
T F 15. <u>Leprechaun</u> ultimately derives from the Latin base CORPOR-, CORP(US)-.

6. Words of Interest. Supply the appropriate word from the list below.

1. widemouthed pitcher   _____

2. violent windstorm   _____

3. skillful; dexterous   _____

4. to meddle in a harmful
    manner   _____

5. funereal hymn   _____

6. garment that lends support   _____

7. portable cloth shelter   _____

8. the trappings or privileges
    of royalty   _____

9. easing of tensions between
    nations   _____

10. emotional characteristics   _____

11. a bouquet of flowers worn
    at the wrist or shoulder   _____

12. one who leases a building
    or property   _____

13. clothing; apparel   _____

14. embarrassing mishap   _____

15. game played with rackets   _____

adroit	dirge	temperament
contretemps	dress	tempest
corsage	ewer	tenant
corset	regalia	tennis
détente	tamper	tent

7. <u>TEND-, TENT-, TENS-</u>

    Match each word with the best definition.*

    ____ 1. attendance   A. purpose
    ____ 2. contention   B. the state of being expanded:
    ____ 3. distention   dilation
    ____ 4. extension   C. affectation
    ____ 5. intention   D. competition
    ____ 6. portent   E. a granting of extra time to
    ____ 7. pretense   complete a project
    ____ 8. superintendence   F. the act of supervising
                                  G. omen
                                  H. the act of being present

    *The verbs that correspond to these nouns end in -tend:
    <u>attend</u>, <u>contend</u>, etc.

8. **Review:** Indicate whether the following pairs are synonyms or
    antonyms by circling S or A.

    S A   1. visionary   - practical
    S A   2. trivial   - significant
    S A   3. recluse   - extrovert
    S A   4. inadvertently   - unintentionally
    S A   5. auspicious   - ominous
    S A   6. punctilious   - careful
    S A   7. prohibit   - allow
    S A   8. accent   - stress
    S A   9. equanimity   - sangfroid
    S A 10. inert   - active
    S A 11. tenor   - purport
    S A 12. curative   - remedy
    S A 13. contrary   - agreeable
    S A 14. travail   - labor
    S A 15. carnival   - Mardi gras

9. **Review:** From your knowledge of Latin bases, try to supply the appropriate word before referring to the list of possible answers at the end of the exercise.

1. Social scientists describe a person who is "turned inward" as an _____ and one who is "turned outward" as an _____ .

2. A person who "exchanges" his or her clothes for those of the opposite sex is called a _____ .

3. A club that is _____ "shuts out" certain people.

4. Extraterrestrials are also called _____ because it is assumed that they will be strange or different from earthlings.

5. A cautious person who "looks all around" before acting is described as _____ .

6. Etymologically, an _____ is an exclamatory, obscene word that "fills out" a person's vocabulary.

7. A place where sick or weak people are cared for is called an _____ .

8. The adjective _____ applies to sociable persons who like to be part of a "flock" of people.

9. The noun _____ , the act of leading one astray, usually is used of sexual enticement.

10. A person who is "full of holiness," i.e., hypocritically devout, is described as _____ .

11. The noun _____ refers to an occupation or calling. The noun _____ , on the other hand, generally refers to something that calls a person away from what he normally does, in other words, a hobby.

12. In a court of law, a person who lies under oath is guilty of _____ .

13. The word _____ , which etymologically means "foot of a crane," is a synonym for <u>lineage</u>.

14. A homophone of <u>fort</u>, which means "a person's strong point," is _____ .

15. The adjective _____ can refer to someone traveling on foot as well as to something ordinary or commonplace.

16. One who is _____ is multi-talented; such a person is "capable of being turned" in many ways.

17. A synonym for <u>world</u>, which etymologically means "a turning as one," is _____.

18. A problem so "thoroughly folded or tangled" that it is baffling can be described as _____.

19. The adjectives <u>allusive</u>, <u>elusive</u>, and <u>illusive</u> are sometimes confused. _____ means "evasive"; _____ means "deceptive"; _____ means "indirectly referred to."

20. A synonym for "to copy," which etymologically means "to fold twice," is _____.

aliens

avocation

circumspect

duplicate

exclusive

expletive

extrovert

forte

gregarious

infirmary

introvert

pedestrian

pedigree

perjury

perplexing

sanctimonious

seduction

transvestite

universe

versatile

vocation

10. **Review:** Supply the missing letters to form an Anglo-Saxon equivalent of each Latinate word.

    1.   fortress   s _ _ _ _ _ hold

    2.   grade (n.)   s _ _ _

    3.   injure   w _ _ _ _

    4.   gravity   h _ _ _ _ ness

    5.   optimum   b _ _ _

    6.   plenitude   f _ _ _ ness

    7.   primary   f _ _ _ _

    8.   sacred   h _ _ _

    9.   verbose   w _ _ _ y

   10. vocation   c _ _ _ ing

11. **Review:** Indicate whether each statement is true or false by circling T or F.

T F   1.   The <u>praying</u> <u>mantis</u> derives its name from its reverent posture.

T F   2.   An <u>envoy</u> (also spelled <u>envoi</u>) is a literary postscript.

T F   3.   <u>Onion</u> ultimately derives from the Latin base UND-.

T F   4.   <u>Complexion</u> once was a synonym for "temperament."

T F   5.   <u>Ferry</u> ("to convey over water") derives from the Latin base FER-.

T F   6.   Originally, <u>pioneer</u> referred to a foot soldier who cleared the wilderness for an army.

T F   7.   <u>Produce</u> (fresh fruits and vegetables) derives from a metaphor, "that which the earth brings forth."

T F   8.   The etymological meaning of <u>inert</u> is "lifeless."

T F   9.   <u>Souvenir</u> (< sub- + VEN-) means "to remember" in French.

T F 10. <u>Prudent</u> derives from the Latin base PRUD- ("excessively modest") + the suffix -ent.

LESSON IX

1.   Adjective-forming Suffixes. Circle the prefixes (if any),
     bases, and suffixes and give the meanings of the following
     words.

   1. aquatic   _____

   2. bilateral   _____

   3. consentaneous _____

   4. corpulent   _____

   5. domestic   _____

   6. grandiose   _____

   7. habitual   _____

   8. ingenious   _____

   9. pedestrian   _____

  10. plenary   _____

  11. rectilinear   _____

  12. senile   _____

  13. servile   _____

  14. temporary   _____

2. Words of Interest. Supply the appropriate word from the list below.

Word	Etymological Meaning	Current Meaning
1. _____	clever invention	locomotive
2. _____	a monastic hood	a game-piece with spots
3. _____	removal of the dishes	last course of a meal
4. _____	a stop on horseback	a public promenade
5. _____	a breathing upon	divine inspiration
6. _____	the light-bearer	Satan
7. _____	flame	a large, gregarious wading bird
8. _____	lordship	a prison
9. _____	puffed up	a baked dish made of eggs
10. _____	a house	hemispherical roof
11. _____	blazing	shocking; notorious
12. _____	to illuminate a manuscript	to depict
13. _____	having flame-like curves	highly ornate
14. _____	side by side	security for a loan
15. _____	separated	a few

afflatus	engine	limn
collateral	flagrant	Lucifer
dessert	flamboyant	parade
dome	flamenco	pawn
domino	flamingo	several
dungeon	ingenuity	soufflé

3. DOM(IN)-; FLAG(R)-, FLAM(M)-; LUC-, LUMIN-; PAR-; SEN-; SERV-

   Match each word with the best definition.

   ____ 1. condominium   A. large, destructive fire
   ____ 2. dominant   B. attire
   ____ 3. domain   C. to assist in a minor capacity
   ____ 4. domicile   D. self-restrained
   ____ 5. conflagration   E. priority gained through length
   ____ 6. illuminate   of service
   ____ 7. pellucid   F. place of residence
   ____ 8. parry   G. to deflect; to evade
   ____ 9. pare   H. to enlighten
   ____ 10. apparel   I. to remove by cutting
   ____ 11. seniority   J. realm
   ____ 12. senectitude   K. pre-eminent
   ____ 13. subserve   L. slavery
   ____ 14. reserved   M. old age
   ____ 15. servitude   N. a purchased apartment
                                 O. clear

4. Indicate whether each statement is true or false by circling T
   or F.

   T F   1. Flammable and inflammable are opposite in meaning.
   T F   2. Einstein was a luminary in the field of physics.
   T F   3. The etymology of Dominican is can[es] + Domini, "hounds
             of the Lord."
   T F   4. Originality and cleverness are characteristic of an
             ingenuous idea.
   T F   5. Sire ultimately derives from the Latin SEN-.
   T F   6. "A madam" and "madam" are titles that may be used
             interchangeably to refer to any woman.
   T F   7. The word lunatic illustrates a once commonly held
             belief that phases of the moon affect a person's
             behavior.
   T F   8. Gin (the alcoholic liquor) derives from the Latin base
             GEN-.
   T F   9. The etymology of danger is "a lord's jurisdiction."
   T F 10. The etymological meaning of lucubration is close to the
             expression "burning the midnight oil."

61

5. GEN-, GENER-; GEN-

    Match each word with the best definition.

    ___ 1. congenital   A. agreeable
    ___ 2. genre   B. offspring; descendant
    ___ 3. disingenuous   C. to begin to grow; to sprout
    ___ 4. gender   D. selfish
    ___ 5. gentle   E. unselfish
    ___ 6. progeny   F. mild
    ___ 7. generalize   G. native
    ___ 8. congenial   H. existing at birth
    ___ 9. indigenous   I. classification as to sex
    ___ 10. generous   J. capable of being produced
    ___ 11. regenerate   K. category of artistic composition
    ___ 12. generic products   L. goods sold by type or kind,
    ___ 13. genuine   not by brand name
    ___ 14. genetics   N. to produce anew
    ___ 15. germinate   O. to make universal or indefinite
                                P. the science of heredity
                                Q. insincere; calculating
                                R. authentic

6. Review: The French Connection. From the list below supply
    the base from which each word derives.

    1. align   _____

    2. vis-à-vis   _____

    3. ingredient   _____

    4. attendance   _____

    5. egalitarian   _____

    6. regime   _____

    7. damsel   _____

    8. enclosure   _____

    9. grievous   _____

    10. portion   _____

11. convey   _____

12. revenue   _____

13. dissemble   _____

14. ponder   _____

15. abound   _____

CLUD-, CLUS-   REG-, (RIG-), RECT-
DOM(IN)-   SIMIL-, SIMUL-
EQU-, (IQU-)   TEND-, TENT-, TENS-
GRAD-, GRESS-   UND-
GRAV-   VEN-, VENT-
LINE-   VI(A)-
PART-   VID-, VIS-
PEND-, PENS-

7.   **Review:** Circle the letter of the word that does not mean the
     same as the other two.

1.   (A) vista   7.   (A) comply
     (B) venue   (B) transgress
     (C) view   (C) observe

2.   (A) comprehension   8.   (A) equivocal
     (B) recompense   (B) equivalent
     (C) compensation   (C) similar

3.   (A) priority   9.   (A) finale
     (B) precedence   (B) finial
     (C) preview   (C) conclusion

4.   (A) semiannual   10. (A) deference
     (B) biennial   (B) respect
     (C) biannual   (C) deferment

5.   (A) ponderous   11. (A) ingenuity
     (B) pendulous   (B) complicity
     (C) grave   (C) inventiveness

6.   (A) pusillanimous   12. (A) pliant
     (B) magnanimous   (B) supple
     (C) benevolent   (C) suppliant

13. (A) egress
    (B) regress
    (C) degenerate

14. (A) limn
    (B) temper
    (C) delineate

15. (A) generate
    (B) produce
    (C) purvey

16. (A) precede
    (B) prevent
    (C) preclude

17. (A) accede
    (B) assent
    (C) proceed

18. (A) secure
    (B) detain
    (C) fortify

19. (A) improvised
    (B) extemporaneous
    (C) contretemps

20. (A) separate
    (B) habitual
    (C) individual

21. (A) spite
    (B) malice
    (C) redoubt

22. (A) redound
    (B) unite
    (C) combine

23. (A) luminous
    (B) flagrant
    (C) perspicuous

24. (A) revelry
    (B) parapet
    (C) rampart

LESSON X

1. <u>SAL-, (SIL-), SALT-, (SULT-)</u>

   Match each word with its <u>etymological</u> meaning.

   ____ 1. insult
   ____ 2. assail
   ____ 3. resilient
   ____ 4. salacious
   ____ 5. salmon
   ____ 6. salience
   ____ 7. sally (n.)
   ____ 8. exultation
   ____ 9. desultory
   ____10. result

   A. a fish that leaps
   B. leaping from one topic to the next: random
   C. fond of leaping: lecherous
   D. a witty remark
   E. the consequence of leaping back
   F. to leap at: attack
   G. the act of leaping vigorously: rejoicing
   H. to jump on someone: to offend
   I. capable of leaping back after a mishap
   J. a striking point: one that leaps out at you

2. Choose the correct answer by circling A or B.

   1. obligatory: (A) recumbent   (B) incumbent

   2. excessive: (A) inordinate   (B) subordinate

   3. capable of becoming: (A) potential   (B) potable

   4. to tranquilize: (A) sedate   (B) reside

   5. primitive: (A) ordinal   (B) primordial

   6. powerfulness: (A) potency   (B) pottage

   7. disagreement: (A) dissidence   (B) residence

   8. a broad, deep dish: (A) terrene   (B) tureen

   9. additional pay given
       to a performer: (A) residuals   (B) residue

10. allied: (A) confederate   (B) confident

11. diligent: (A) assiduous   (B) insidious

12. intrinsic: (A) incoherent   (B) inherent

13. treachery: (A) fealty   (B) perfidy

14. to make secondary: (A) suborn   (B) subordinate

15. to remove a body
    from the earth: (A) disinter   (B) deter

3. Words of Interest. Supply the appropriate word from the list
   below.

	Word	Etymological Meaning	Current Meaning
1.	_____	power	a small force with legal authority
2.	_____	lacking faith	timid; shy
3.	_____	to lie on	to sit on eggs in order to hatch them
4.	_____	a sitting (by the enemy)	blockade
5.	_____	a leaping over	acrobatic movement in which the body makes a full revolution
6.	_____	a sitting	a meeting of spiritualists
7.	_____	sleeping compartment	carrel
8.	_____	demon thought to lie on women in their sleep	nightmare
9.	_____	to sit in power	to own; to control

Word	Etymological Meaning	Current Meaning
10. _____	faithful	canine appellation
11. _____	baked earth	fired clay used for roofing tiles, pottery, etc.
12. _____	food that leaps as it cooks	food cooked in a small amount of fat
13. _____	one promised	man engaged to be married
14. _____	to put in the earth	to bury a dead body
15. _____	a beginning	introduction to a discourse

concubine   Fido   Rover
cubicle   incubate   sauté
diffident   incubus   séance
exordium   inter   siege
fiancé   posse   somersault
fiancée   possess   terra cotta

4. Indicate whether each statement is true or false by circling T or F.

T F 1. The etymological meaning of terrier is "earth-dog."
T F 2. The word venom derives from the base VEN-, VENT-.
T F 3. A retrospective view looks to the future.
T F 4. A confidant is a person who can be trusted to keep secrets.
T F 5. Those suffering from extreme acrophobia are likely to keep their feet planted on terra firma.
T F 6. A succuba is the female counterpart of an incubus.
T F 7. Testimony ultimately derives from the Latin base TERR-.
T F 8. The etymology of candidate reflects the notion that a person running for political office should be "pure."
T F 9. The etymology of salad is "leaping or tossed" vegetables.
T F 10. Debonair and genteel similarly reflect the idea of nobility or good breeding.

5. <u>CUMB-, CUB-; FID-; FIDEL-; HER-, HES-; ORD(IN)-;</u>
   <u>POT-, POSS-; SED-, (SID-), SESS-; TERR-</u>

   Match each word with the best definition.

   ___ 1. succumb   A. city in Indiana located
   ___ 2. covey   on high ground
   ___ 3. concubine   B. exceedingly powerful
   ___ 4. defiant   C. a flock of birds
   ___ 5. fiduciary   D. to yield to a superior force
   ___ 6. affiance   E. meeting during which a particular
   ___ 7. adhesive (n.)   activity takes place
   ___ 8. coherence   F. rebellious
   ___ 9. coordinate   G. to pledge in marriage
   ___10. extraordinary   H. person to whom property is en-
   ___11. impotent   trusted for another's benefit
   ___12. session   I. remarkable
   ___13. subsidy   J. logical connection in thought
   ___14. supersede   K. a grant of money
   ___15. Terre Haute   L. powerless
                              M. in some polygamous societies,
                                  a second wife
                              N. glue, for example
                              O. to supplant
                              P. bondsman
                              Q. to place in harmonious relation

6. **Review:** Supply the missing prefix or base.

   1. to enlighten   il _ _ _ _ _ ate

   2. bodily   _ _ _ _ _ _ eal

   3. powerless   _ _ potent

   4. watery   _ _ _ eous

   5. to beget   _ _ _ _ _ ate

   6. slavish   _ _ _ _ ile

   7. heavy with child   _ _ _ _ id

8. earthly   _ _ _ _ estrial

9. kingly   _ _ _ al

10. home   _ _ _ icile

11. combustible   in _ _ _ _ _ able

12. lasting for a short
    time only   t _ _ _ _ _ ary

13. a singing back; re-
    traction   _ _ cantation

14. a yearly record of
    events   _ _ _ als

15. without care   se _ _ _ e

7. Review: Choose the correct answer by circling A or B.

1. native: (A) indigenous   (B) indigent

2. to escort: (A) convoy   (B) convey

3. contest between
   two persons: (A) dual   (B) duel

4. prayerful: (A) precarious   (B) precatory

5. impromptu: (A) contemporary   (B) extempore

6. dead body: (A) corps   (B) corpse

7. forebear: (A) primogenitor   (B) primogeniture

8. immunity: (A) sanctum   (B) sanctuary

9. natural inclination: (A) preponderance (B) propensity

10. to betroth: (A) affiance   (B) finance

11. final dinner course: (A) desert   (B) dessert

12. pertaining to pro-
    creation: (A) genital   (B) gentile

69

13. one's strong point: (A) fort   (B) forte

14. maliciousness: (A) respite   (B) spite

15. to gather together: (A) assemble   (B) assimilate

16. clever: (A) ingenuous   (B) ingenious

17. tenet: (A) principal   (B) principle

18. countenance: (A) visage   (B) visa

19. offspring: (A) progeny   (B) prodigy

20. diplomatic agent: (A) envy   (B) envoy

8. **Review:** Indicate whether the following pairs are synonyms or antonyms by circling S or A.

S	A	1.	temporal	-	carnal
S	A	2.	flagrant	-	scandalous
S	A	3.	endanger	-	imperil
S	A	4.	purvey	-	provide
S	A	5.	succedent	-	prior
S	A	6.	confident	-	self-possessed
S	A	7.	controvert	-	oppose
S	A	8.	resilient	-	supple
S	A	9.	unique	-	singular
S	A	10.	separate	-	sever
S	A	11.	inflated	-	swollen
S	A	12.	charm	-	fascinate
S	A	13.	excursus	-	digression
S	A	14.	assured	-	diffident
S	A	15.	habitual	-	customary
S	A	16.	parasol	-	umbrella
S	A	17.	disproportion	-	balance
S	A	18.	repair	-	restore
S	A	19.	parent	-	originate
S	A	20.	imperative	-	optional

LESSON XI

1. Indicate whether the following pairs are synonyms or antonyms by circling S or A.

    S A 1. docile   - intractable
    S A 2. contiguous   - adjacent
    S A 3. train   - retinue
    S A 4. trace   - hint
    S A 5. fallacious   - veracious
    S A 6. confess   - deny
    S A 7. moderate   - extreme
    S A 8. tangent   - digression
    S A 9. mutable   - constant
    S A 10. retreat   - sanctum
    S A 11. accredit   - certify
    S A 12. commute   - exchange
    S A 13. miscreant   - infidel
    S A 14. doctrine   - tenet
    S A 15. contingency - certainty

2. <u>TRACT-</u>

    Match each word with the best definition.*

    ___ 1. abstract   A. disparagement
    ___ 2. attraction   B. written agreement
    ___ 3. contract   C. recantation
    ___ 4. detraction   D. charm
    ___ 5. distraction   E. deduction
    ___ 6. extraction   F. a lengthening
    ___ 7. protraction   G. diversion
    ___ 8. retraction   H. summary
    ___ 9. subtraction   I. lineage

    *The verbs that correspond to these nouns end in -tract: <u>abstract</u>, <u>attract</u>, <u>contract</u>, etc.

71

Part I, Lesson XI

3. Words of Interest. Supply the appropriate word from the list below.

1. legendary   _____

2. a coward   _____

3. contemporary   _____

4. foot-soldiery   _____

5. to accord as a favor   _____

6. whole; entire   _____

7. a fixture for drawing
    liquids   _____

8. moderate estimation of
    one's abilities   _____

9. a contribution of income
    to support a government   _____

10. lit. a false step:
     social blunder   _____

11. a low cabinet or cupboard   _____

12. a distinguishing feature   _____

13. to shed an outer covering   _____

14. discernment of the
     esthetically superior   _____

15. failure to fulfill an
     obligation   _____

commode	grant	molt
default	infantry	recreant
fabulous	integral	taste
faucet	modern	tax
faux pas	modesty	trait

4. FA(B)-, FAT-, FESS-, FAM-

    Match each word with its _etymological_ meaning.

    ___ 1. infamous   A. to speak with: chat
    ___ 2. fame   B. mythical goddess related to Fate
    ___ 3. nefarious   C. easy to speak to: pleasant
    ___ 4. fate   D. what is said about a person:
    ___ 5. infant   public reputation
    ___ 6. fatal   E. having a bad reputation
    ___ 7. affable   F. to take away one's
    ___ 8. fairy   good reputation: malign
    ___ 9. defame   G. unspeakable: wicked
    ___ 10. confabulate   H. pertaining to bad fate:
                                   causing death
                               I. that which is said
                                   or decreed: destiny
                               J. one who cannot speak: baby

5. Indicate whether each statement is true or false by circling T
    or F.

    T F   1. A _credulous_ person tends to be skeptical about the
               statements of others.
    T F   2. The word _treat_ belongs to the TRACT- family of words.
    T F   3. _Juggernaut_ originally referred to the Hindu god
               Krishna.
    T F   4. A _tactful_ person handles situations delicately so as to
               maintain harmonious relations.
    T F   5. A person who is tenacious is persistent; but a person
               who is _pertinacious_ is extremely persistent, hence
               stubborn.
    T F   6. Etymologically, _rehearse_ means "to harrow again."
    T F   7. The etymological meaning of _doctor_ is "teacher."
    T F   8. Etymologically, _maintain_ means "to keep in hand."
    T F   9. A person who speaks in a _desultory_ fashion "leaps" from
               one topic to the next.
    T F 10. The medical term for a female fatality of an automobile
               accident is _femme fatale_.

6. **Review:** The French Connection. From the list below supply
    the base from which each word derives.

    1. deuce   _____

    2. gendarme   _____

    3. embellish   _____

    4. point   _____

    5. sewer   _____

    6. premier   _____

    7. limn   _____

    8. séance   _____

    9. accredit   _____

    10. defiant   _____

    11. serf   _____

    12. détente   _____

    13. ensure   _____

    14. employ   _____

    15. ounce   _____

    AQU(A)-   PLIC-, PLEX-
    BENE-, BON-   POT-, POSS-
    CANT-, (CENT-)   PRIM-
    CRED-   PUNG-, PUNCT-
    CUR-   SED-, (SID-), SESS-
    DU-   SERV-
    FID-   TEN-, (TIN-), TENT-
    GEN-   UN-
    LUC-, LUMIN-

7. **Review:** Circle the letter of the word that does not mean the same as the other two.

1. (A) execration
    (B) malignancy
    (C) imprecation

2. (A) unprejudiced
    (B) perspicacious
    (C) impartial

3. (A) digress
    (B) deviate
    (C) deprecate

4. (A) supplication
    (B) complicity
    (C) collusion

5. (A) segregate
    (B) assemble
    (C) convene

6. (A) evoke
    (B) expedite
    (C) educe

7. (A) corpulent
    (B) plenitudinous
    (C) redundant

8. (A) prelude
    (B) introduction
    (C) counterpoise

9. (A) perverse
    (B) applicable
    (C) unpliable

10. (A) accomplice
    (B) accessory
    (C) malefactor

11. (A) pedestrian
    (B) provident
    (C) prosaic

12. (A) tenet
    (B) dispensation
    (C) doctrine

13. (A) occlude
    (B) expunge
    (C) annul

14. (A) intervene
    (B) intercross
    (C) intercede

15. (A) simultaneous
    (B) contemporary
    (C) omnipotent

16. (A) proportion
    (B) proceed
    (C) progress

17. (A) avouch
    (B) affirm
    (C) aggregate

18. (A) apparel
    (B) habiliments
    (C) entreaty

19. (A) attract
    (B) magnetize
    (C) revert

20. (A) confabulation
    (B) ordinance
    (C) conversation

8. **Review:** Food. Match each word with the base from which it derives.

___	1. onion	A.	BENE-, BON-
___	2. bonbon	B.	BI-, BIN-
___	3. dessert	C.	CRUC-
___	4. tenderloin	D.	FLAG(R)-, FLAM(M)-
___	5. salmon	E.	FLAT-
___	6. flambé	F.	MOD-
___	7. hot cross bun	G.	SAL-, (SIL-), SALT-, (SULT-)
___	8. biscuit	H.	SERV-
___	9. soufflé	I.	TEND-, TENT-, TENS-
___	10. à la mode	J.	UN-

9. **Review:** Identify the prefixes from which the following words derive.

1. country   _____

2. superb   _____

3. interior   _____

4. preposterous   _____

5. ancient   _____

6. rear   _____

7. outrage   _____

8. soprano   _____

LESSON XII

1. Using your knowledge of Latin elements, answer the following
    items.

    1. Trees whose leaves "fall down" annually are called:
        (A) deciduous (B) defoliants (C) defunct

    2. A star that rapidly grows in brilliance and then fades is
        called a(n): (A) nova (B) meteorite (C) asteroid

    3. Manufacture etymologically means _____.

    4. Which of the following words can mean "reddish"?
        (A) fervid (B) flowery (C) florid (D) fervent

    5. Someone who does all kinds of work is called a:
        (A) malfeasant (B) defeatist (C) factotum

    6. What medical practice attempts to cure illness by
        "puncturing with a needle"? (A) biofeedback
        (B) vivisection (C) acupuncture

    7. If docile means "teachable," what does facile mean
        etymologically? _____.

    8. Why is "the Occident" another name for "the West"?
        _____.

    9. Are the homophones flower and flour etymologically
        related? _____.

    10. All of the following words have to do with "sharpness."
        Which one refers to mental keenness? (A) acumen
        (B) acrimony (C) acidity (D) acerbity

    11. Something that "flows like honey" (a sweet-sounding
        voice, for example) is said to be: (A) mellivorous
        (B) mellifluous (C) melliferous

    12. To what Latin base is fetish related? _____.

    13. Which of the following words does not belong to the CAD-,
        (CID-), CAS- family? (A) chance (B) parachute
        (C) cadet (D) decadence

14. Someone who is "flowing" with wealth is said to be:
(A) magnanimous (B) affluent (C) munificent

15. Explain the difference between the verbs <u>affect</u> and <u>effect</u>.
_____
_____
_____
_____

16. A disease that once was thought to be caused by the "influence" of the heavenly bodies is called:
(A) bubonic plague (B) influenza (C) malaria

17. A person whose speech "flows readily," especially in a foreign language, is said to be: (A) logorrheic (B) fluent (C) eloquent

18. Which of the following words does not belong to the FAC-family? (A) deface (B) efface (C) edifice (D) preface

19. Small bits of colored paper thrown at ticker-tape parades are called: (A) confetti (B) comfits (C) confections

20. The heading of an article or document that catches a person's attention is called: (A) caitiff (B) caption (C) cable

2. <u>CAP-, (CIP-), CAPT-, (CEPT-)</u>

Match each word with the best definition.

____ 1. anticipate   A. idea; notion
____ 2. emancipate   B. seizure and control of an area
____ 3. concept   C. to become pregnant
____ 4. inception   D. to free
____ 5. intercept   E. spacious
____ 6. conceive   F. easily affected emotionally
____ 7. deception   G. a beginning
____ 8. capacious   H. fraud
____ 9. occupation   I. to cut off from a destination
____10. susceptible   J. to expect; to foresee

3. <u>FAC-, (FIC-), FACT-, (FECT-)</u>

Match each word with the best definition.

____ 1. satisfaction	A. fondness
____ 2. proficiency	B. to wipe out; to destroy
____ 3. feature (v.)	C. discontent
____ 4. affectation	D. an aspect or phase
____ 5. deficit	E. pretension; airs
____ 6. interface	F. seditious
____ 7. efface	G. skill; ability
____ 8. superficial	H. to make better
____ 9. factious	I. program designed to communicate
____10. feasible	information from one computer
____11. facet	to another
____12. disaffection	J. gratification
____13. discomfiture	K. confusion; embarrassment
____14. counterfeit	L. to give prominence to
____15. affection	M. capable of being done
	N. shortage
	O. shallow
	P. forgery
	Q. to suppress

4. Circle the letter of the word that does not mean the same as the other two.

1. (A) affluent
    (B) facilitative
    (C) abundant

2. (A) defect
    (B) efficacy
    (C) fault

3. (A) exacerbate
    (B) aggravate
    (C) evoke

4. (A) incidence
    (B) incumbency
    (C) occurrence

5. (A) redundant
    (B) superfluous
    (C) superannuated

6. (A) adroit
    (B) acrid
    (C) pungent

7. (A) feat
    (B) regimen
    (C) exploit

8. (A) corpse
    (B) cadaver
    (C) corps

9.   (A) provenance
    (B) preconception
    (C) prejudice

10. (A) capacity
    (B) deciduousness
    (C) ability

11. (A) facsimile
    (B) facetiousness
    (C) replica

12. (A) infectious
    (B) contagious
    (C) redintegrative

13. (A) factitious
    (B) artificial
    (C) factious

14. (A) pernicious
    (B) internecine
    (C) fated

15. (A) captivate
    (B) charm
    (C) besiege

16. (A) incorrigible
    (B) incredible
    (C) inconceivable

17. (A) temporarily
    (B) coincidently
    (C) simultaneously

18. (A) fallacious
    (B) deceptive
    (C) ineffable

19. (A) occasion
    (B) concurrence
    (C) event

20. (A) decadence
    (B) degeneration
    (C) delineation

21. (A) munificence
    (B) generosity
    (C) avoirdupois

22. (A) plenty
    (B) superficiality
    (C) sufficiency

23. (A) captious
    (B) modern
    (C) novel

24. (A) innocent
    (B) ingenuous
    (C) culpable

5. Words of Interest. Supply the appropriate word from the list below.

1. the principal house on a landed estate _____

2. a type of peach _____

3. to defraud _____

4. female member of a royal family _____

5. to deprive of virginity   _____

6. a portable case for carrying
    loose sheets of paper   _____

7. a fever marked by chills   _____

8. an umbrella-like device
    that opens midair and
    guards against a fall   _____

9. lit. sour wine   _____

10. something annoying or
    offensive   _____

11. set of instructions
    for making a food dish   _____

12. incompetent; lazy   _____

13. to regain health   _____

14. to provide food and service
    for a large party   _____

15. impatiently expectant   _____

ague	feckless	portfolio
cater	hacienda	princess
cheat	nectarine*	recipe
deflower	nuisance	recover
eager	parachute	vinegar

*Related to the NEC-, NIC- base.

6. Supply the missing base.

1. to make new again   re _ _ _ ate

2. harmless   in _ _ _ uous

3. leafage   _ _ _ _ age

4. waterfall   _ _ _ cade

5. harmful   _ _ _ ious

6. a place where things
    are made   _ _ _ _ ory

7. keenness of perception   _ _ _ men

8. continued flow   f _ _ _

9. bearing flowers   _ _ _ _ iferous

10. to take prisoner   _ _ _ _ ure

7. **Review:** Indicate whether the following pairs are synonyms or antonyms by circling S or A.

S   A   1. preface   -   exordium
S   A   2. impedimenta -   obstacles
S   A   3. accidental   -   adventitious
S   A   4. deceit   -   duplicity
S   A   5. profit   -   benefit
S   A   6. superfluity -   surfeit
S   A   7. defame   -   malign
S   A   8. dubious   -   certain
S   A   9. florid   -   ornate
S   A 10. integrity   -   completeness
S   A 11. fashion   -   mold
S   A 12. salient   -   inconspicuous
S   A 13. tact   -   diplomacy
S   A 14. sedate   -   impassioned
S   A 15. casual   -   formal

8.   **Review:** In the following two exercises, circle the bases and then match each word with the best definition.

___ 1.   seniority   A.   general agreement

___ 2.   reservoir   B.   supplies

___ 3.   countenance   C.   priority

___ 4.   obloquy   D.   face

___ 5.   quintessence   E.   to disapprove strongly

___ 6.   provisions   F.   a place where something is saved

___ 7.   excursus   G.   digression

___ 8.   consensus   H.   damage to one's reputation

___ 9.   closet   I.   small room used for storage

___10.   deprecate   J.   the fifth and supreme element

                    *   *   *

___ 1.   subordinate   A.   undetermined

___ 2.   compunction   B.   stimulating

___ 3.   deplete   C.   illness

___ 4.   corrective   D.   subservient

___ 5.   provocative   E.   to yield

___ 6.   mutual   F.   tending to make right or straight

___ 7.   effectual   G.   producing a desired result

___ 8.   succumb   H.   to drain

___ 9.   pending   I.   reciprocal

___10.   malady   J.   scruple

9. **Review:** Supply the missing letters to form an Anglo-Saxon equivalent of each Latinate word.

    1. domicile   h _ _ _

    2. genus   k _ _ _

    3. credible   b _ _ _ _ _ able

    4. terrestrial   e _ _ _ _ ly

    5. illuminate   en _ _ _ _ _ en

    6. similar   l _ _ _

    7. sentiment   f _ _ _ ing

    8. vision   s _ _ _ _

    9. incorporate   em _ _ _ _

    10. fable   t _ _ _

10. **Review:** Indicate whether each statement is true or false by circling T or F.

T   F   1. Bimillenary refers to a period of 2000 years.
T   F   2. Double entendre, a type of wordplay, never has risqué overtones.
T   F   3. Excruciate originally referred to the punishment of crucifixion.
T   F   4. An infidel is a disloyal friend.
T   F   5. Molt is a member of the MUT- family of words.
T   F   6. Although manufactured goods are made by machine, the etymology of manufacture is "to make by hand."
T   F   7. Senate owes its derivation to the fact that this Roman council originally was composed of elders.
T   F   8. Before the time of Julius Caesar, the Roman calendar consisted of 355 days.
T   F   9. Semicentennial refers to a 75th anniversary.
T   F   10. Benediction pertains to speech characterized by extremely meticulous pronunciation.

LESSON XIII

1. ## FUS-

    Match each word with the best definition.*

    ___ 1. confuse
    ___ 2. defuse
    ___ 3. effuse
    ___ 4. infuse
    ___ 5. interfuse
    ___ 6. refuse
    ___ 7. suffuse
    ___ 8. transfuse

    A. to inspire; to introduce
    B. to overspread with liquid
    C. to deny
    D. to perplex; to confound
    E. to pour out; to exude
    F. to intermingle; to blend one
        with another
    G. to transfer from one source
        to another
    H. to deprive of intent to harm

    *The nouns that correspond to these verbs end in -fusion:
    confusion, effusion, etc. (The verb defuse lacks a noun
    counterpart.)

2. Indicate whether the following pairs are synonyms or antonyms
    by circling S or A.

    S A   1. native   -   foreign
    S A   2. decomposition -   decay
    S A   3. tortuous   -   winding
    S A   4. apposite   -   relevant
    S A   5. dispel   -   assemble
    S A   6. refuse   -   trash
    S A   7. torment   -   suffering
    S A   8. extortionate   -   excessive
    S A   9. pregnant   -   meaningful
    S A 10. postpone   -   defer
    S A 11. opponent   -   ally
    S A 12. expound   -   explain
    S A 13. duress   -   coercion
    S A 14. distort   -   misrepresent
    S A 15. appealing   -   repulsive

3.   Words of Interest. Supply the appropriate word from the list below.

	Word	Etymological Meaning	Current Meaning
1.	_____	hard	sullen; gloomy
2.	_____	something twisted	a portable light
3.	_____	rebirth	period of revival of humanistic learning
4.	_____	secret-keeper	clerical worker
5.	_____	a twisted chain	twisted metal collar worn by ancient Gauls and Britons
6.	_____	later born; younger	weak; insignificant
7.	_____	accusation	unlawful activity
8.	_____	nose-twister	a plant with pungent leaves and seeds
9.	_____	pouring (easily)	ineffectual; useless
10.	_____	agreement	public performance of music
11.	_____	a setting down or aside	railroad or bus station
12.	_____	decision	an order having the force of law
13.	_____	natural	unsophisticated
14.	_____	something twisted back	witty reply

concert   futile   Renaissance
crime   naïve   retort
decree   nasturtium   secretary
depot   peal   torch
dour   puny   torque

4. POSE-

Match each word with the best definition.

___ 1. compose	A.	to levy (a tax); to obtrude upon
___ 2. depose	B.	to put forward: to offer
___ 3. expose	C.	to conjecture
___ 4. impose	D.	to put down: to overthrow
___ 5. juxtapose	E.	to lay open to view
___ 6. oppose	F.	to create; to fashion
___ 7. propose	G.	to place above something
___ 8. repose	H.	to lie at rest
___ 9. superimpose	I.	to set against: to resist
___10. suppose	J.	to place side by side (for comparison)

5. PEL(L)-, PULS-

Supply the appropriate prefix.*

1. to drive forward   _____ pel

2. to drive out   _____ pel

3. to drive back   _____ pel

4. to drive on or against   _____ pel

5. to drive together
    forcibly   _____ pel

*The nouns that correspond to these verbs end in -pulsion or
-pulse: compulsion, impulsion, impulse, etc.; adjectives
generally end in -pulsive: compulsive, impulsive, etc.

6. Circle the prefixes, bases, and suffixes and then give the meaning of each element.

MEANINGS

1. contingent _____

2. adventitious _____

3. retentive _____

4. prelusory _____

5. immutable _____

6. adherent _____

7. docile _____

8. credulous _____

9. inordinate _____

10. infantile _____

11. vociferant _____

12. leonine _____

13. accurate _____

14. turbid _____

15. pertinacious _____

7. <u>CERN-, CRET-, [CERT-]</u>

Match each word with the best definition.

___ 1.	ascertain	A.	prudence
___ 2.	certain	B.	to throw into confusion
___ 3.	certificate	C.	to determine
___ 4.	concern	D.	jumbled
___ 5.	disconcert	E.	countercharge
___ 6.	discretion	F.	anxiety; manufacturing company
___ 7.	excrete	G.	mystery
___ 8.	indiscriminate	H.	a diploma, for example
___ 9.	recrimination	I.	sure
___10.	secret	J.	to eliminate from the body

8. **Review:** Supply the missing prefix or base.

1. unmistakable   in _ _ _ _ ible

2. tale   _ _ ble

3. manner   _ _ _ e

4. touchable   _ _ _ _ ible

5. foreword   _ _ _ face

6. a genetic change   _ _ _ ation

7. new   _ _ _ el

8. slavery   _ _ _ _ itude

9. birth   _ _ _ ivity

10. righteousness   _ _ _ _ itude

11. unbelievable   _ _ credible

12. conduit for water   aque _ _ _ _

13. word-for-word   _ _ _ _ atim

14. to harden   in _ _ _ ate

15. teachings   _ _ _ _ rine

9. **Review:** The French Connection. From the list below supply the base from which each word derives.

1. push   _____

2. genteel   _____

3. fealty   _____

4. ordain   _____

5. assess   _____

6. puissance   _____

7. assault   _____

8. grant   _____

9. catch   _____

10. fault   _____

11. retreat   _____

12. nee   _____

13. eager   _____

14. flourish   _____

15. fairy   _____

AC(U)-, ACR-, ACET-	NASC-, NAT-
CAP-, (CIP-), CAPT-, (CEPT-)	ORD(IN)-
	PEL(L)-, PULS-
CRED-	POT-, POSS-
FA(B)-, FAT-, FESS-, FAM-	SAL-, (SIL-), SALT-, (SULT-)
FALL-, FALS-	
FIDEL-	SED-, (SID-), SESS-
FLOR-	TRACT-
GEN-	

LESSON XIV

1. To show how the following words have undergone degeneration of meaning, give both their original and current meanings.

		ORIGINAL MEANING	CURRENT MEANING
1.	cheat	_____	_____
2.	counterfeit	_____	_____
3.	egregious	_____	_____
4.	officious	_____	_____
5.	plausible	_____	_____
6.	sanctimony	_____	_____
7.	silly	_____	_____
8.	vile	_____	_____

The following words have undergone elevation of meaning. Give both their original and current meanings.

9.	count (= nobleman)	_____	_____
10.	engineer	_____	_____
11.	frank	_____	_____
12.	naughty	_____	_____
13.	nice	_____	_____
14.	pioneer	_____	_____
15.	president	_____	_____
16.	rapture	_____	_____

Part I, Lesson XIV

2. AM-; DE-, DIV-; [JOURN-]; OR-; PROB-, [PROV-]; RAP-, RAPT-, (REPT-); STRING-, STRICT-, [STRAIN-]; VER-

Circle the bases in the following words and then match each with the best definition.

___ 1.	amicable	A.	to suspend until another time
___ 2.	amorous	B.	to affirm
___ 3.	deify	C.	swift
___ 4.	divination	D.	condemnation
___ 5.	adjourn	E.	exacting
___ 6.	adore	F.	the power of a god: prophecy
___ 7.	inexorable	G.	grasping
___ 8.	reprove	H.	appearance of the truth
___ 9.	probity	I.	to scold
___10.	disapprobation	J.	to make into a god
___11.	rapacious	K.	full of love
___12.	rapid	L.	inquiry
___13.	surreptitious	M.	integrity; rectitude
___14.	restrain	N.	performed secretly
___15.	strict	O.	unyielding
___16.	verisimilitude	P.	to hold back; to check
___17.	aver	Q.	to demonstrate again
		R.	friendly
		S.	to revere

92

3.   Words of Interest.   Supply the appropriate word from the list
     below.

     1.   female lead in an opera   _____

     2.   anguish of mind or body   _____

     3.   scoundrel   _____

     4.   to transport with delight   _____

     5.   nonprofessional   _____

     6.   shrine consecrated to a   _____
          prophetic god

     7.   day-to-day record of   _____
          personal experiences

     8.   judgment; decision   _____

     9.   to reside temporarily   _____

    10.   Chinese idol   _____

    11.   illicit lover   _____

    12.   a fudge confection   _____
          "next to heaven"

    13.   farewell   _____

    14.   influential status   _____

    15.   lit. with a round mouth: _____
          rich in sound; bombastic

          adieu   enrapture   paramour
          amateur   joss   prestige
          distress   journal   reprobate
          diva   oracle   sojourn
          divinity   orotund   verdict

4. **Review:** Circle the letter of the word that does not mean the same as the other two.

1. (A) bona fide
   (B) genuine
   (C) pretentious

2. (A) discretion
   (B) confabulation
   (C) circumspection

3. (A) insidious
   (B) fabulous
   (C) incredible

4. (A) defer
   (B) adjudicate
   (C) postpone

5. (A) excruciate
   (B) torture
   (C) defame

6. (A) tractable
   (B) docile
   (C) dilatory

7. (A) counterpoise
   (B) discompose
   (C) perturb

8. (A) certify
   (B) confirm
   (C) probe

9. (A) congenial
   (B) punctilious
   (C) affable

10. (A) conductor
    (B) accomplice
    (C) confederate

11. (A) intervene
    (B) imprecate
    (C) interpose

12. (A) tenable
    (B) tenacious
    (C) adhesive

13. (A) distort
    (B) pervert
    (C) pertain

14. (A) naïve
    (B) innocent
    (C) disingenuous

15. (A) component
    (B) ingredient
    (C) tort

16. (A) confuse
    (B) replenish
    (C) perplex

17. (A) discernment
    (B) continence
    (C) perception

18. (A) transmute
    (B) juxtapose
    (C) convert

19. (A) eloquent
    (B) elusive
    (C) fluent

20. (A) dominant
    (B) preponderant
    (C) obdurate

REVIEW OF LESSONS VIII-XIV

1. Indicate whether each statement is true or false by circling T or F.

T F   1. A <u>womanizer</u> may be involved concurrently with several paramours.

T F   2. <u>Omnium-gatherum</u> is a synonym for <u>hodgepodge</u>.

T F   3. <u>Corps</u> is a literary term referring to a body of poetry.

T F   4. <u>Nice</u> has undergone degeneration of meaning.

T F   5. A <u>compulsive</u> person has irresistible urges to do certain things.

T F   6. The word <u>fame</u> originally referred to any report.

T F   7. Words associated with the country often undergo elevation of meaning.

T F   8. The word <u>disease</u> once referred to any discomfort.

T F   9. <u>Salacious</u> derives from the Latin base SAL-, SALT-.

T F 10. Generalization and specialization are types of semantic change.

T F 11. Originally, <u>plausible</u> meant "worthy of applause."

T F 12. <u>Sir</u>, <u>señor</u>, and <u>monsieur</u> all derive from the Latin base SEN-.

T F 13. <u>Prestige</u> (originally "juggler's tricks") has undergone elevation of meaning.

T F 14. Being able to recognize the Latin elements in an English word is an infallible way to determine its current meaning.

T F 15. <u>Found</u> ("to establish") and <u>found</u> ("to melt metal") derive from the same Latin base.

2. Match each suffix with its meaning.

____ 1. -ity   A. full of

____ 2. -ible   B. = ing

____ 3. -ary   C. state of; quality of

____ 4. -ose   D. one connected with

____ 5. -ant, -ent, (-ient)   E. able to be; tending to

3. Indicate whether the following pairs are synonyms or antonyms by circling S or A.

S A	1.	ravish	-	deflower
S A	2.	journal	-	diary
S A	3.	compound	-	combine
S A	4.	affluent	-	impecunious
S A	5.	adherent	-	renegade
S A	6.	detain	-	advance
S A	7.	result	-	consequence
S A	8.	acrimony	-	bitterness
S A	9.	maladroit	-	clumsy
S A	10.	flammable	-	inflammable
S A	11.	reprove	-	censure
S A	12.	torch	-	flambeau
S A	13.	confident	-	sanguine
S A	14.	servile	-	regal
S A	15.	recumbency	-	repose

4. Occupations. Match each word with the base from which it derives.

___ 1.	rector	A. CAD-, (CID-), CAS-
___ 2.	servant	B. CERN-, CRET-
___ 3.	plenipotentiary	C. CRED-
___ 4.	president	D. DOC-, DOCT-
___ 5.	doctor	E. DOM(IN)-
___ 6.	postmistress	F. FAC-, (FIC-), FACT-, (FECT-)
___ 7.	manufacturer	G. FLOR-
___ 8.	parachutist	H. GEN-
___ 9.	florist	I. ORD(IN)-
___10.	secretary	J. PON-, POSIT-
___11.	entertainer	K. POT-, POSS-
___12.	orderly	L. REG-, (RIG-), RECT-
___13.	domestic	M. SED-, (SID-), SESS-
___14.	engineer	N. SERV-
___15.	creditor	O. TEN-, (TIN-), TENT-

5. Supply the missing base.

1. newborn   neo _ _ _ e

2. person taken (prisoner)   _ _ _ _ ive

3. god-like   _ _ _ ine

4. newness   _ _ _ elty

5. tending to believe   _ _ _ _ ulous

6. truthful   _ _ _ acious

7. speech   _ _ ation

8. having equal sides   equi _ _ _ _ _ al

9. enlightenment   il _ _ _ _ _ ation

10. unchangeable   im _ _ _ able

11. to throb   _ _ _ _ ate

12. place   p _ _ _ _ ion

13. full of love   _ _ orous

14. unlike   dis _ _ _ _ _ ar

15. foreword   pre _ _ ce

16. to embody   in _ _ _ _ _ _ ate

17. to blow into   in _ _ _ _ e

18. full of leaves   _ _ _ _ ose

19. lasting   _ _ _ able

20. indeed   in f _ _ _ (two words)

6. Circle the bases in the following words and then match each
with the best definition.

___ 1.	terrace	A.	mutually ruinous
___ 2.	casualty	B.	to bear; to suffer patiently
___ 3.	retract	C.	temperate
___ 4.	endure	D.	accompanying
___ 5.	confederacy	E.	deck; balcony
___ 6.	degenerate	F.	slight
___ 7.	moderate	G.	treachery
___ 8.	tenuous	H.	to recant
___ 9.	aqua	I.	to deteriorate
___10.	fallacious	J.	machine
___11.	apparatus	K.	disagreeable; offensive
___12.	attendant	L.	person killed or missing in action
___13.	obnoxious	M.	alliance
___14.	perfidy	N.	false
___15.	internecine	O.	light greenish blue

LESSON XV

1. CID-, CIS-; MATR-, MATERN-; PATRI-; SEQU-, SECUT-; SOL-; VIV-

    Match each word with the best definition.

    ____ 1. excise   A. servile attentiveness
    ____ 2. concise   B. to cut out
    ____ 3. incision   C. succeeding
    ____ 4. matriculate   D. succinct
    ____ 5. expatriate   E. to harass
    ____ 6. execution   F. food
    ____ 7. prosecute   G. significant
    ____ 8. persecute   H. the act of cutting into
    ____ 9. subsequent   I. graphic
    ____10. consequential   J. to enroll in college
    ____11. obsequiousness   K. to institute legal proceedings
    ____12. solitaire   L. to outlive
    ____13. victuals   M. card game played alone
    ____14. vivid   N. the act of putting to death
    ____15. survive   O. to banish from one's country

2. Match each word with the best definition.

    ____ 1. fratricide   A. baby-killer
    ____ 2. genocide   B. brother-killer
    ____ 3. homicide   C. sister-killer
    ____ 4. infanticide   D. father- or mother-killer
    ____ 5. insecticide   E. wife-killer
    ____ 6. parricide   F. insect eradicator
    ____ 7. regicide   G. self-killer
    ____ 8. sororicide   H. killer of another human being
    ____ 9. suicide   I. king-killer
    ____10. uxoricide   J. extermination of an entire
                                     racial or national group

3. Words of Interest. Supply the appropriate word from the list below.

	Word	Etymological Meaning	Current Meaning
1.	_____	it does not follow	illogical inference
2.	_____	stone cuttings	anything that binds or unites
3.	_____	rapid recital of Pater Nosters	a comedian's rapid speech
4.	_____	to father (a deed)	to commit a crime
5.	_____	an exact cut	summary
6.	_____	a person who follows or pursues	a man courting a woman
7.	_____	things to be lived on	a choice dish
8.	_____	procession of mourners to the grave	funeral rites
9.	_____	pertaining to a banquet	sociable
10.	_____	little cutting tool	tool used to cut stone
11.	_____	member of the origi-nal Roman aristocracy	any person of noble or high rank
12.	_____	alone	gloomy; surly

cement	non sequitur	précis
chisel	patrician	scissors
convivial	patter	suitor
exequies	perpetrate	sullen
glue	perpetuate	viand

4. __MATR-, MATERN-; PATR-, PATERN-; PATRI-; PATRON-__

Form the feminine equivalent of each of the following words by substituting the base MATR-, MATERN- for PATR-, PATERN-; PATRI-; PATRON-. Then give the meanings of both. (Each pair is not necessarily parallel in meaning.)

MEANING

1. patrilineal _____

    _____ _____

2. patriarch _____

    _____ _____

3. patronymic _____

    _____ _____

4. paternal _____

    _____ _____

5. paternity _____

    _____ _____

6. patricide _____

    _____ _____

7. patrimony _____

    _____ _____

8. patron _____

    _____ _____

5. Indicate whether each statement is true or false by circling T
    or F.

T   F   1. Prequel, a recent addition to the English language, is
            modeled on sequel.
T   F   2. A Caesarean section is so called because Julius Caesar
            reputedly was born this way.
T   F   3. A person who kills a parrot is guilty of parricide.
T   F   4. In the expression, "she's a beauty," the word beauty
            has shifted from a concrete to an abstract meaning.
T   F   5. Pattern derives from the Latin base PATRON-.
T   F   6. Cadaver belongs to the CID-, CIS- family of words.
T   F   7. The word hussy was once simply a variant of
            "housewife."
T   F   8. The etymological meaning of assassin is "eater of
            corned beef hash."
T   F   9. The etymological meaning of second is "that which
            follows."
T   F   10. Courtesan has undergone degeneration of meaning;
            originally the word referred to a lady of the court.

6. **Review**: Circle the letter of the word that best fits the
    definition.

    1. slanderous: (A) affable
                                 (B) defamatory
                                 (C) ineffable
                                 (D) nefarious

    2. to divert: (A) abstract
                                 (B) distract
                                 (C) extract
                                 (D) subtract

    3. sway: (A) affluence
                                 (B) confluence
                                 (C) effluence
                                 (D) influence

    4. to betray: (A) conceive
                                 (B) deceive
                                 (C) perceive
                                 (D) receive

5. to expand:

    (A) attend
    (B) contend
    (C) distend
    (D) portend

6. to contaminate:

    (A) affect
    (B) effect
    (C) infect
    (D) perfect

7. occurrence:

    (A) cadence
    (B) coincidence
    (C) decadence
    (D) incidence

8. ugly:

    (A) compulsive
    (B) expulsive
    (C) propulsive
    (D) repulsive

9. to place side by side:

    (A) appose
    (B) compose
    (C) depose
    (D) expose

10. a witty reply:

    (A) distortion
    (B) extortion
    (C) retort
    (D) tort

11. to confine:

    (A) compound
    (B) expound
    (C) impound
    (D) propound

12. to lie at rest:

    (A) juxtapose
    (B) oppose
    (C) propose
    (D) repose

13. recovery:

    (A) anticipation
    (B) occupation
    (C) participation
    (D) recuperation

14. deprivation of occupancy:

    (A) dispossession
    (B) possession
    (C) prepossession
    (D) repossession

15. to assist in carrying out:
   (A) conserve
   (B) observe
   (C) preserve
   (D) subserve

16. to wield:
   (A) apply
   (B) imply
   (C) ply
   (D) reply

17. to agree:
   (A) concur
   (B) incur
   (C) occur
   (D) recur

18. to reveal:
   (A) close
   (B) disclose
   (C) enclose
   (D) foreclose

19. to accomplish:
   (A) complement
   (B) compliment
   (C) implement
   (D) supplement

20. entreaty:
   (A) complication
   (B) explication
   (C) implication
   (D) supplication

21. to esteem:
   (A) expect
   (B) inspect
   (C) respect
   (D) suspect

22. refreshment:
   (A) affection
   (B) confection
   (C) infection
   (D) refection

23. to bewilder:
   (A) confuse
   (B) diffuse
   (C) infuse
   (D) perfuse

24. to scold:
   (A) approve
   (B) disprove
   (C) prove
   (D) reprove

Part I, Lesson XV

7. **Review:** In the following two exercises, circle the bases and then match each word with the best definition.

_____ 1. aversion   A. humorous

_____ 2. decide   B. obsolete; old-fashioned

_____ 3. superannuated   C. disposition

_____ 4. confine   D. a beginning

_____ 5. temper   E. to make up one's mind

_____ 6. luminous   F. infirmity of old age

_____ 7. inception   G. dislike

_____ 8. acetic   H. bright; clear

_____ 9. facetious   I. pertaining to vinegar

_____10. senility   J. to restrict

*   *   *

_____ 1. inflammatory   A. to interfere

_____ 2. intrude   B. grotesque imitation

_____ 3. spectacle   C. dangerous

_____ 4. pretentious   D. suitability

_____ 5. execrate   E. affected

_____ 6. precarious   F. unruffled; serene

_____ 7. expediency   G. accidental; nonessential

_____ 8. imperturbable   H. to curse

_____ 9. travesty   I. provocative

_____10. adventitious   J. entertaining or unusual exhibit

105

8.   **Review:** The French Connection. Match each word with the base
     from which it derives.

____	1.	quarantine	A. AC(U)-, ACR-, ACET-
____	2.	succor	B. CLUD-, CLUS-
____	3.	grandeur	C. CRUC-
____	4.	voice	D. CUR(R)-, CURS-
____	5.	levee	E. FID-
____	6.	enclosure	F. GEN-
____	7.	detain	G. GRAND-
____	8.	repair	H. LEV-
____	9.	crucial	I. PATRI-
____	10.	revenue	J. PREC-
____	11.	faith	K. QUADR(U)-
____	12.	regulate	L. REG-, (RIG-), RECT-
____	13.	gentry	M. TEN-, (TIN-), TENT-
____	14.	ague	N. VEN-, VENT-
____	15.	prayer	O. VOC-, VOK-

9.   **Review:** Match each word with its <u>etymological</u> meaning.

____	1.	matrimony	A. to sit in power
____	2.	punctuate	B. a lord's jurisdiction
____	3.	possess	C. military group made up of
____	4.	insult	young men
____	5.	funnel	D. a holy place
____	6.	semester	E. to mark off with dots
____	7.	genie	F. take a little of this and
____	8.	probable	a little of that
____	9.	danger	G. a list of words
____	10.	infantry	H. to leap on
____	11.	tax	I. hard
____	12.	recipe	J. likely to prove true
____	13.	dour	K. a period of six months
____	14.	sanctuary	L. a government's touching of
____	15.	vocabulary	the pocketbook
			M. guardian spirit
			N. little object for pouring
			O. sanctioned motherhood

LESSON XVI

1. Circle the letter of the word that best fits the definition.

1. discriminating:

    (A) collective
    (B) elective
    (C) selective

2. to command:

    (A) adjoin
    (B) disjoin
    (C) enjoin

3. determined:

    (A) absolute
    (B) dissolute
    (C) resolute

4. able to pay debts:

    (A) insolvent
    (B) soluble
    (C) solvent

5. abnormal growth:

    (A) crescendo
    (B) excrescence
    (C) increase

6. to bring "under the yoke":

    (A) conjoin
    (B) conjugate
    (C) subjugate

7. to caution:

    (A) admonish
    (B) demonstrate
    (C) remonstrate

8. bias:

    (A) predilection
    (B) recollection
    (C) selection

9. connecting word:

    (A) conjunction
    (B) injunction
    (C) junction

10. wandering:

    (A) itinerant
    (B) obituary
    (C) perishable

11. an answer in reply:

    (A) adjunctive
    (B) injunction
    (C) rejoinder

12. outcome: (A) initiative
                                           (B) issue
                                           (C) transit

13. person or thing that warns: (A) monitor
                                           (B) monstrosity
                                           (C) monument

14. accompanying: (A) concomitant
                                           (B) conjugal
                                           (C) conjunctive

15. worthy of being chosen: (A) electoral
                                           (B) eligible
                                           (C) intellectual

2. Words of Interest. Supply the appropriate word from the list below.

	Word	Etymological Meaning	Current Meaning
1.	_____	new growth	newly enlisted soldier
2.	_____	something to be read	myth
3.	_____	companion (to a king)	European nobleman
4.	_____	a warning (from the gods)	hideous creature
5.	_____	chosen body of soldiers	Roman military unit
6.	_____	council	faction that controls a government after a revolution
7.	_____	reminder of great deeds	memorial
8.	_____	military increase or reinforcement	all personnel manning a ship
9.	_____	chosen people	select group
10.	_____	carelessly draped	woman's nightgown

	Word	Etymological Meaning	Current Meaning
11.	_____	pertaining to "getting hitched"	marital
12.	_____	a gathering together	series of connected spirals
13.	_____	a going around for votes	desire for fame, rank, or power
14.	_____	the act of going apart from established authority	rebellion
15.	_____	coming up secretly	unforeseen; quick

ambition   elite   monument
coil   junta   muster
conjugal   legend   negligee
count   legion   recruit
crew   legume   sedition
cull   monster   sudden

3. Indicate whether the following pairs are synonyms or antonyms by circling S or A.

S A 1. concrete - actual
S A 2. adjunct - assistant
S A 3. legible - readable
S A 4. negligible - significant
S A 5. dissolute - debauched
S A 6. initiate - instruct
S A 7. illegal - lawful
S A 8. summon - dismiss
S A 9. accrue - decrease
S A 10. solution - explanation

4. I-, IT-

Match each word with the best definition.

___	1.	ambience	A. route of a journey
___	2.	circuitous	B. short-lived
___	3.	commence	C. roundabout; indirect
___	4.	exit	D. notice of a person's death
___	5.	county	E. environment
___	6.	initial	F. to die
___	7.	itinerary	G. to begin
___	8.	issue	H. stupor; ecstasy
___	9.	obituary	I. the act of going out
___	10.	perish	J. originally, territory of a count
___	11.	trance	K. first letter of a name
___	12.	transitory	L. crux

5. Review: The following words have entered English through
   Spanish. Match each word with the base from which it derives.

___	1.	adios	A. AM-
___	2.	hacienda	B. DE-, DIV-
___	3.	amigo	C. DOM(IN)-
___	4.	sombrero	D. FAC-, (FIC-), FACT-, (FECT-)
___	5.	duenna	E. FLAG(R)-, FLAM(M)-
___	6.	flamingo	F. HOM- ("man")
___	7.	señor	G. JUG-, JUNCT-
___	8.	junta	H. PATR-, PATERN-
___	9.	hombre	I. SEN-
___	10.	padre	J. UMBR- ("shade")

6. **Review:** In the following two exercises, circle the bases and then match each word with the best definition.

___ 1.	engender	A. to compromise to gain time
___ 2.	exposé	B. blackmail
___ 3.	refuse (n.)	C. fawning
___ 4.	temporize	D. to force
___ 5.	astringent	E. cosmetic that constricts the pores of the skin
___ 6.	compel	
___ 7.	turbulent	F. garbage
___ 8.	extortion	G. unruly; agitated
___ 9.	concerted	H. to give rise to; to produce
___10.	obsequious	I. disclosure
		J. planned in agreement

* * *

___ 1.	occasion	A. obligatory
___ 2.	defector	B. to stick together
___ 3.	advertise	C. deserter
___ 4.	capacious	D. hostile; assertive
___ 5.	pendulum	E. flowing with honey
___ 6.	cohere	F. event
___ 7.	indifferent	G. spacious
___ 8.	incumbent (adj.)	H. something that swings back and forth from one course to another
___ 9.	aggressive	
___10.	mellifluous	I. uninterested; apathetic
		J. to call attention to a product

111

7. **Review:** Circle the letter of the word in each group that does
    not mean the same as the others.

1. (A) contrary
    (B) opposite
    (C) unimpeded
    (D) converse

2. (A) intercede
    (B) intervene
    (C) interface
    (D) interpose

3. (A) delineate
    (B) divert
    (C) portray
    (D) limn

4. (A) adherence
    (B) fidelity
    (C) fealty
    (D) feasibility

5. (A) accept
    (B) countenance
    (C) assess
    (D) approve

6. (A) tangent
    (B) digression
    (C) discrimination
    (D) excursion

7. (A) confound
    (B) supersede
    (C) perplex
    (D) confuse

8. (A) defame
    (B) malign
    (C) prepossess
    (D) traduce

9. (A) elucidate
    (B) expend
    (C) expound
    (D) explicate

10. (A) parent
    (B) progenitor
    (C) progeny
    (D) ancestor

11. (A) tenet
    (B) principle
    (C) doctrine
    (D) recidivism

12. (A) credulous
    (B) veritable
    (C) genuine
    (D) bona fide

13. (A) features
    (B) lineaments
    (C) traits
    (D) perspectives

14. (A) decomposition
    (B) disaffection
    (C) decay
    (D) disintegration

15. (A) convoke
    (B) muster
    (C) convene
    (D) contrast

16. (A) prelusive
    (B) protrusive
    (C) introductory
    (D) prefatory

17. (A) alert
    (B) veracious
    (C) animated
    (D) vivacious

18. (A) corpulent
    (B) plentiful
    (C) bounteous
    (D) abundant

LESSON XVII

1. FERV-; FRANG-, (FRING-), FRACT-; GRAN-; MINOR-, MINUS-,
MINUT-; QUIR-, QUISIT-, QUEST-; SEC-, SEG-, SECT-

Match each word with the best definition.

___ 1.	fervency	A.	something obligatory
___ 2.	defray	B.	a natural division
___ 3.	refrain	C.	to behave with affected elegance
___ 4.	refract	D.	to "break back" light
___ 5.	granite	E.	to question
___ 6.	granulated	F.	investigation
___ 7.	minutiae	G.	a written order for something
___ 8.	mince	H.	to be nauseated
___ 9.	acquisition	I.	trifling details
___10.	requisition	J.	enthusiasm; zeal
___11.	query (v.)	K.	a recurring phrase or verse
___12.	inquisition	L.	a grainy, igneous rock
___13.	requirement	M.	formed into grains
___14.	vivisection	N.	dissection of a live animal
___15.	segment	O.	to pay
		P.	something gained
		Q.	curiosity

2. Consult a dictionary (if necessary) in order to determine the etymological and current meanings of each of the following diminutives.

1. armadillo _____

2. chapel _____

3. closet _____

4. cubicle _____

5. curriculum _____

6. granule _____

7. homunculus _____

8. jugular _____

9. morsel _____

10. muscle _____

11. oracle _____

12. oriole _____

13. punctilio _____

14. pupil _____

15. umbrella _____

3. Indicate whether the following pairs are synonyms or antonyms by circling S or A.

```
S  A   1.  fervor          -   passion
S  A   2.  infringe        -   encroach
S  A   3.  administer      -   execute
S  A   4.  diminutive      -   huge
S  A   5.  fragile         -   sturdy
S  A   6.  inquisitive     -   curious
S  A   7.  fractious       -   quarrelsome
S  A   8.  diminish        -   increase
S  A   9.  fragmentary     -   whole
S  A  10.  garner          -   accumulate
S  A  11.  dissect         -   analyze
S  A  12.  require         -   forgo
S  A  13.  questionnaire   -   survey
S  A  14.  ingrain         -   infuse
S  A  15.  frailty         -   susceptibility
```

4. Words of Interest. Supply the appropriate word from the list below.

  1. "voting with shards":
      the right to vote   _____

  2. an invertebrate with sharply
      marked body features   _____

  3. gemstone   _____

  4. shell filled with explosives   _____

  5. "bone-crusher":
      fish-eating hawk   _____

  6. ornamental work of
      delicate design   _____

  7. "seedy apple": a fruit
      containing many seeds   _____

  8. slow, stately dance   _____

  9. tool that cuts tall grass   _____

 10. of special excellence
      or beauty   _____

 11. medieval musician   _____

 12. detailed list of entrees   _____

     exquisite   insect   osprey
     filigree   menu   pomegranate
     garnet   minstrel   sickle
     grenade   minuet   suffrage

5. Supply the missing base.

1. to cut in two   bi _ _ _ _

2. a mixture of cereal, nuts, and
    fruit served for breakfast   _ _ _ _ ola

3. a seeking   q _ _ _ _

4. fellow-feeling   com _ _ _ _ ion

5. to bubble   ef _ _ _ _ esce

6. place where grain is stored   _ _ _ _ ary

7. a break   _ _ _ _ _ ure

8. lacking feeling or emotion   im _ _ _ _ ive

9. the smaller part   _ _ _ _ _ ity

10. a doctor's client   _ _ _ _ ent

6. Indicate whether each statement is true or false by circling T
    or F.

T F 1. Villain orignally signified a farm laborer.
T F 2. Etymologically, commencement exercises celebrate not
          the conclusion but the beginning of a graduate's
          career.
T F 3. A saturnine temperament is characterized by
          unpredictable changes of mood.
T F 4. Pencil originally meant "little feather."
T F 5. Although perish and decedent derive from different
          Latin bases, they share the idea of "permanent
          departure."
T F 6. Liquor once referred to any liquid.
T F 7. The adjective conjugal loosely corresponds to the
          modern notion of "getting hitched."
T F 8. The drink sangría is named for its blood-red color.
T F 9. The diminutive scruple means "pebble."
T F 10. Gladiolus derives its etymology from its "glad" or
          cheerful appearance.

7. **Review:** Supply the missing base.

1.	truthfulness	_ _ _ acity
2.	like	_ _ _ _ _ ar
3.	lively	_ _ _ acious
4.	friendship (among nations)	_ _ ity
5.	readable	_ _ _ ible
6.	"on the dot"	_ _ _ _ _ ual
7.	forewarning	pre _ _ _ ition
8.	care of the hands	mani _ _ _ e
9.	fatherly	_ _ _ _ _ _ al
10.	lawful	_ _ _ al
11.	the act of speaking alone	_ _ _ iloquy
12.	sharp	_ _ _ te
13.	motherhood	_ _ _ _ _ _ ity
14.	touching	_ _ _ _ ent
15.	to ask	in _ _ _ _ e

8. **Review:** Occupations. Match each word with the base from which it derives.

___ 1. journalist	A. ALIEN-
___ 2. courier	B. CAP-, (CIP-), CAPT-, (CEPT-)
___ 3. director	C. CUR(R)-, CURS-
___ 4. advocate	D. [JOURN-]
___ 5. executive	E. DUC-, DUCT-
___ 6. alienist	F. EQU-, (IQU-)
___ 7. minister	G. FIRM-
___ 8. farmer	H. JUDIC-
___ 9. equilibrist	I. LEG-, (LIG-), LECT-
___10. caterer	J. MINOR-, MINUS-, MINUT-
___11. producer	K. PON-, POSIT-
___12. composer	L. REG-, (RIG-), RECT-
___13. senator	M. SEN-
___14. judge	N. SEQU-, SECUT-
___15. legislator	O. VOC-, VOK-

9. **Review:** The following words have entered English through Italian. Match each with the Latin base from which it derives.

___ 1. segue	A. CAD-, (CID-), CAS-
___ 2. cadenza	B. CRE-, CRESC-, CRET-
___ 3. novella	C. DE-, DIV-
___ 4. replica	D. FAC-, (FIC-), FACT-, (FECT-)
___ 5. tempo	E. FLU-, FLUX-, FLUOR(O)-, FLUV-
___ 6. influenza	F. FOLI-
___ 7. umbrella	G. NOV-
___ 8. diva	H. PLIC-, PLEX-
___ 9. confetti	I. PUNG-, PUNCT-
___10. improvisatore	J. SEQU-, SECUT-
___11. solo	K. SOL-
___12. portfolio	L. TEMPER-, TEMPOR-
___13. terra cotta	M. TERR-
___14. crescendo	N. UMBR- ("shade")
___15. contrapuntal	O. VID-, VIS-

LESSON XVIII

1. Indicate whether the following pairs are synonyms or antonyms by circling S or A.

S	A	1.	dictum	-	maxim
S	A	2.	valiant	-	cowardly
S	A	3.	agile	-	awkward
S	A	4.	clamorous	-	vociferous
S	A	5.	edict	-	proclamation
S	A	6.	consonance	-	discord
S	A	7.	predicament	-	dilemma
S	A	8.	conditional	-	provisional
S	A	9.	prodigal	-	frugal
S	A	10.	conscientious	-	painstaking
S	A	11.	prevalent	-	widespread
S	A	12.	cogitate	-	ponder
S	A	13.	congeries	-	aggregation
S	A	14.	resonant	-	orotund
S	A	15.	redaction	-	revision

2. **GER-, GEST-**

   Match each word with the best definition.*

   ____ 1. congest   A. to propose
   ____ 2. digest   B. to excrete
   ____ 3. egest   C. to assimilate
   ____ 4. ingest   D. to overcrowd
   ____ 5. suggest   E. to take in by swallowing

   *The nouns that correspond to these verbs end in -gestion: congestion, digestion, etc.; digest can function as both noun and verb.

3. VAL-, [VAIL-]

Match each word with the best definition.

___ 1.	convalescence	A.	priceless
___ 2.	invaluable	B.	to compensate for
___ 3.	valuable	C.	same
___ 4.	ambivalent	D.	to make use of
___ 5.	equivalent	E.	simultaneously attracted to and repulsed from
___ 6.	countervail	F.	the process of recovering one's health
___ 7.	evaluate	G.	sound; effective
___ 8.	valid	H.	to estimate
___ 9.	devalue	I.	of considerable monetary worth
___ 10.	avail	J.	to reduce the worth of

4. Words of Interest. Supply the appropriate word from the list below.

	Word	Etymological Meaning	Current Meaning
1.	_____	the act of speaking ill of	a curse
2.	_____	Christian martyr	sentimental card sent on February 14th
3.	_____	driving in both directions	capable of multiple interpretations
4.	_____	waging war	hostile
5.	_____	a saying farewell	farewell address at commencement
6.	_____	wordbook	lexicon
7.	_____	what is put on the table	untidy condition
8.	_____	the act of carrying	pregnancy
9.	_____	something truly said	decision of a jury

	Word	Etymological Meaning	Current Meaning
10.	_____	deed; exploit	joke; taunt
11.	_____	to release from one's hand	to free from bondage
12.	_____	something sent	communication through an intermediary
13.	_____	to drive a ship	to traverse the sea or air
14.	_____	pertaining to health	an invalid
15.	_____	little song	poem of 14 lines

ambiguous   jest   register
belligerent   malediction   sonnet
dictionary   manumit   valediction
fustigate   mess   Valentine
gerund   message   valetudinarian
gestation   navigate   verdict

5. CLAM-, [CLAIM-]

Match each word with the best definition.*

____ 1. acclaim   A. to renounce
____ 2. declaim   B. to recover lost articles
____ 3. disclaim   C. to interject
____ 4. exclaim   D. to announce publicly
____ 5. proclaim   E. to applaud enthusiatically
____ 6. reclaim   F. to recite for rhetorical effect

*The nouns that correspond to these verbs end in -clamation:
acclamation, declamation, etc.; acclaim can function as both
noun and verb.

In the following two exercises, match each word with the best definition.

6. <u>DIC-, DICT-</u>

___ 1. condition	A.	denial; inconsistency
___ 2. prediction	B.	to point out
___ 3. dictation	C.	to duplicate
___ 4. contradiction	D.	the addressing of a literary work to someone
___ 5. dedication	E.	the act of uttering words to be transcribed
___ 6. indicate	F.	act motivated by vengeance
___ 7. vendetta	G.	enunciation
___ 8. ditto (v.)	H.	stipulation
	I.	a simple song
	J.	a forecast

7. <u>MIT(T)-, MIS(S)-</u>

___ 1. missive	A.	to allow entrance
___ 2. demise	B.	officer in charge
___ 3. commissary	C.	to conjecture
___ 4. surmise (v.)	D.	the state of being bound to a course of action
___ 5. compromise	E.	a letter
___ 6. noncommital	F.	prayer book
___ 7. premise	G.	death
___ 8. admit	H.	agreement reached by mutual concession
___ 9. commitment	I.	a lessening of degree
___10. omission	J.	proposition from which a conclusion is drawn
___11. remission	K.	to yield to another
___12. submit	L.	not having a particular view
	M.	military supply store
	N.	neglect

122

8. **Review:** Circle the letter of the word in each group that does not mean the same as the others.

1. (A) pertinent
    (B) continent
    (C) apposite
    (D) relevant

2. (A) dissonant
    (B) dissolute
    (C) perverted
    (D) unprincipled

3. (A) appendage
    (B) accessory
    (C) attraction
    (D) adjunct

4. (A) enjoin
    (B) direct
    (C) order
    (D) elucidate

5. (A) sinecure
    (B) entertainment
    (C) distraction
    (D) diversion

6. (A) coincident
    (B) adventitious
    (C) simultaneous
    (D) contemporaneous

7. (A) edict
    (B) predicament
    (C) proclamation
    (D) decree

8. (A) frail
    (B) fractious
    (C) rebellious
    (D) contentious

9. (A) summon
    (B) convoke
    (C) assemble
    (D) declaim

10. (A) controvert
    (B) dispense
    (C) divide
    (D) apportion

11. (A) prejudice
    (B) preconception
    (C) prepossession
    (D) prevision

12. (A) envoy
    (B) courier
    (C) messenger
    (D) corsair

13. (A) succeed
    (B) supervene
    (C) ensue
    (D) cant

14. (A) resilient
    (B) submissive
    (C) compliant
    (D) tractable

15. (A) ambiguous
    (B) equivocal
    (C) ambitious
    (D) uncertain

16. (A) corrupt
    (B) decayed
    (C) valetudinary
    (D) infected

17. (A) aspect
    (B) feature
    (C) facet
    (D) vista

18. (A) sudden
    (B) abstruse
    (C) unexpected
    (D) rapid

9. **Review:** Food. Match each word with the base(s) from which it derives.

___	1. cauliflower	A.	AC(U)-, ACR-, ACET-
___	2. victuals	B.	AQU(A)-
___	3. mincemeat	C.	BENE-, BON-
___	4. divinity	D.	CAP-, (CIP-), CAPT-, (CEPT-)
___	5. grains	E.	CRE-, CRESC-, CRET-
___	6. confections	F.	DE-, DIV-
___	7. vinegar	G.	DIC-, DICT-
___	8. legumes	H.	FAC-, (FIC-), FACT-, (FECT-)
___	9. aquavit	I.	FLOR-
___	10. compote	J.	GRAN-
___	11. sauté	K.	LEG-, (LIG-), LECT-
___	12. cater	L.	MINOR-, MINUS-, MINUT-
___ ___	13. (eggs) benedict	M.	PAN- ("bread")
___	14. pantry	N.	PON-, POSIT-
___	15. croissant	O.	SAL-, (SIL-), SALT-, (SULT-)
		P.	VIV-

10. **Review:** Indicate whether each statement is true or false by circling T or F.

T F 1. Euphemisms are seldom employed for words and expressions associated with death.

T F 2. The etymological meaning of <u>lavatory</u> is "a place for washing."

T F 3. The etymology of <u>chaplain</u> is "keeper of the rosary."

T F 4. In Shakespeare's day the word <u>deer</u> was a synonym for "animal," especially a small mammal.

T F 5. <u>Sonar</u> is an acronym for "sound navigation ranging."

T F 6. The etymological meaning of <u>disaster</u> is "ill-starred."

T F 7. <u>Fumigate</u> and <u>perfume</u> derive from the same Latin base.

T F 8. The etymology of <u>muscle</u> is "little fly."

T F 9. Originally, a <u>count</u> served as companion to a king.

T F 10. <u>Malingerers</u> are "eager beavers," often volunteering to do additional work.

T F 11. A <u>sinecure</u> is a job entailing few responsibilities.

T F 12. A <u>vitamin</u> is a substance "essential to life."

T F 13. <u>Sanctimonious</u> has undergone elevation of meaning.

T F 14. "To act condescendingly toward" is the meaning of <u>patronize</u>.

T F 15. <u>Flexibility</u> is characteristic of anything stringent.

LESSON XIX

1. SCRIB-, SCRIPT-

Match each word with the best definition.*

___ 1. ascribe   A. to condemn; to prohibit
___ 2. circumscribe   B. to make a written copy of
___ 3. conscript   C. to attribute
___ 4. describe   D. to engrave; to autograph
___ 5. inscribe   E. to support; to append one's
___ 6. prescribe   signature to a document
___ 7. proscribe   F. to enroll for military service
___ 8. subscribe   G. to give an account of
___ 9. superscribe   H. to designate (usu. by a doctor)
___ 10. transcribe   the use of a remedy
                             I. to delimit; to encircle
                             J. to write above or on top of
                                 something

   *The nouns that correspond to these verbs end in -script or
   -scription: ascription, circumscription, conscript,
   conscription, etc.

2. Indicate whether the following pairs are synonyms or antonyms
    by circling S or A.

    S A   1. rest   -   remainder
    S A   2. constant   -   variable
    S A   3. statute   -   edict
    S A   4. nominal   -   significant
    S A   5. exist   -   occur
    S A   6. erratic   -   unconventional
    S A   7. destiny   -   fate
    S A   8. persistent -   obstinate
    S A   9. ejaculate   -   exclaim
    S A 10. extant   -   extinct
    S A 11. objective   -   impartial
    S A 12. instate   -   dismiss
    S A 13. abject   -   despicable
    S A 14. convoluted -   complicated
    S A 15. stationary -   movable

3. Words of Interest. Supply the appropriate word from the list below.

	Word	Etymological Meaning	Current Meaning
1.	_____	a stopping place	unit of verse
2.	_____	a calling by name	system of naming
3.	_____	a roll of writing	one book within a set
4.	_____	(something) thrown	a casting of goods overboard
5.	_____	to write too much	to write in a careless, hurried manner
6.	_____	a naming again	celebrity; fame
7.	_____	a staying of arms	truce
8.	_____	small object that stands in the way	hindrance
9.	_____	a standing over	belief unreasonably supported by faith in magic or chance
10.	_____	something written afterward	message appended to the end of a letter
11.	_____	a turn-face	a reversal; about-face
12.	_____	war name	pseudonym
13.	_____	rolled together	intricate; complicated
14.	_____	a little place for standing	lodging for horses and cattle
15.	_____	to stand with or firm	to have as a price

armistice   obstacle   stable
convoluted   postscript   stanza
cost   renown   steadfast
jettison   scribble   superstition
nom de guerre   scripture   volte-face
nomenclature   solstice   volume

4. <u>ST(A)-, STIT-, SIST-</u>

Match each word with the best definition.

___ 1. constitution   A. a lady or gentleman of the
___ 2. destitute   evening
___ 3. institute   B. an established body of laws;
___ 4. prostitute   physique
___ 5. restitution   C. to replace
___ 6. substitute   D. to establish
                            E. poverty-stricken
                            F. restoration of things to their
                                rightful owner or previous
                                state

Match each verb with the best definition.*

___ 1. assist   A. to cease
___ 2. consist   B. to oppose
___ 3. desist   C. to be composed of
___ 4. insist   D. to exist; to live
___ 5. resist   E. to stand by to help
___ 6. subsist   F. to assert firmly

 *Other verbs that follow this pattern are <u>exist</u> and <u>persist</u>.
 The nouns that correspond to these verbs end in -ance, -ence,
 or -ency: <u>assistance</u>, <u>consistence</u>, <u>consistency</u>, etc.

5. Indicate whether each statement is true or false by circling T or F.

T F 1. Because etymologically <u>ignominious</u> connotes illegitimacy ("having no name"), the word has come to mean "disgraceful" or "shameful."
T F 2. <u>Carnival</u> = "farewell to meat" is an example of a popular etymology.
T F 3. The words <u>male</u> and <u>female</u> are linguistically related.
T F 4. A <u>stallion</u> is so called because it <u>stands</u> in a <u>stall</u> in a <u>stable</u>.
T F 5. <u>Prostitute</u> and <u>obstetrician</u> derive from the Latin base ST(A)-, STIT-.
T F 6. <u>Religious</u> and <u>sacrilegious</u> are etymologically unrelated.
T F 7. The spelling of <u>cockroach</u> has been unaffected by folk etymology.
T F 8. A <u>namesake</u> is a person named in honor of another.
T F 9. <u>Jacket</u> derives from the Latin base JAC-, JECT-.
T F 10. The current meaning of <u>statuesque</u> is "still and emotionless as a three-dimensional image."

6. <u>ERR-; JAC-, JECT-; SCRIB-, SCRIPT-; ST(A)-, STIT-, SIST-; VOLV-, VOLUT-</u>

    Match each word with the best definition.

___ 1. errata	A. a boasting
___ 2. aberration	B. a room for valuables
___ 3. projectile	C. fidgety
___ 4. jactation	D. majestic
___ 5. jut	E. to unfold; to develop
___ 6. escritoire	F. remaining
___ 7. arrest	G. deviation from the normal
___ 8. restaurant	H. to detain in legal custody
___ 9. restive	I. list of errors
___10. stately	J. incident; occurrence
___11. circumstance	K. writing desk
___12. evolve	L. to protrude
___13. voluble	M. a place that serves meals
___14. vault	N. talkative; glib
___15. voluminous	O. missile
	P. large; full
	Q. edible snail

128

7. JAC-, JECT-

    Match each word with the best definition.*

    ____ 1. conjecture   A. to introduce into; to intrude
    ____ 2. deject   B. to throw forward: to predict
    ____ 3. eject   C. to dishearten
    ____ 4. inject   D. to throw out: to expel
    ____ 5. object   E. to rebuff; to discard as useless
    ____ 6. project   F. to cause to undergo something;
    ____ 7. reject   to subjugate
    ____ 8. subject   G. to disapprove; to oppose
                                 H. to guess

    *The nouns that correspond to these verbs end in -ject or
    -jection, with the exception of conjecture.

8. **Review:** The French Connection. Match each word with the base
    from which it derives.

    ____ 1. admonish   A. AM-
    ____ 2. joint   B. CAP-, (CIP-), CAPT-, (CEPT-)
    ____ 3. naïve   C. CED-, CESS-
    ____ 4. lectern   D. GRAN-
    ____ 5. perish   E. I-, IT-
    ____ 6. rampart   F. JUG-, JUNCT-
    ____ 7. adroit   G. LEG-, (LIG-), LECT-
    ____ 8. preview   H. MON-
    ____ 9. misnomer   I. MINOR-, MINUS-, MINUT-
    ____10. assault   J. MIT(T)-, MIS(S)-
    ____11. mess   K. NASC-, NAT-
    ____12. especial   L. NOMEN-, NOMIN-
    ____13. enamor   M. PAR-
    ____14. minstrel   N. PEND-, PENS-
    ____15. proceed   O. REG-, (RIG-), RECT-
    ____16. penthouse   P. SAL-, (SIL-), SALT-, (SULT-)
    ____17. treatise   Q. SPEC-, (SPIC-), SPECT-
    ____18. catch   R. TRACT-
    ____19. grange   S. VID-, VIS-
    ____20. vault   T. VOLV-, VOLUT-

9. **Review:** In the following two exercises, circle the bases and then match each word with the best definition.

___ 1.	regicide	A.	applause
___ 2.	retentive	B.	killer of a king
___ 3.	captivate	C.	bitter; sarcastic
___ 4.	sedentary	D.	to bewitch
___ 5.	cohabitate	E.	paramour
___ 6.	acclaim	F.	requiring much sitting
___ 7.	concubine	G.	page of a book numbered on one side only
___ 8.	folio	H.	having a good memory
___ 9.	firmament	I.	heavens
___10.	acrimonious	J.	to live together

*   *   *

___ 1.	veridical	A.	united into one body
___ 2.	incorporated	B.	short-lived
___ 3.	strict	C.	truthful
___ 4.	unconscionable	D.	childish
___ 5.	resolute	E.	determined
___ 6.	repulsive	F.	contiguous
___ 7.	adjoining	G.	severe; precise
___ 8.	infantile	H.	fabled
___ 9.	legendary	I.	lacking scruples
___10.	transient	J.	disgusting

_____ Name

REVIEW OF LESSONS XV-XIX

1. Indicate whether each statement is true or false by circling T or F.

T F 1. A very <u>superstitious</u> person is unlikely to leave the house for the duration of Friday the 13th.

T F 2. "Fallen woman" is a euphemism for <u>prostitute</u>.

T F 3. Etymologically, the word <u>legion</u> indicates that at one time only the "best" (i.e., "chosen") men were allowed to serve in the Roman army.

T F 4. The word <u>homicide</u> may be used to describe both the crime and its perpetrator.

T F 5. <u>Sanguine</u> is one of several words whose current meaning derives from the humeral theory of physiology.

T F 6. Originally, <u>obstetrician</u> meant "midwife."

T F 7. <u>Awful</u> always has been used in the sense of "very bad" or "dreadful."

T F 8. A querulous <u>valetudinarian</u> is an ideal hospital patient for a candy-striper considering a career in nursing.

T F 9. <u>Suffragette</u> and <u>frail</u> derive from different Latin bases.

T F 10. <u>Legumes</u> derive their name from the fact that they are "collectibles."

T F 11. The word <u>victuals</u> is pronounced as if it were spelled "vittles."

T F 12. As a result of the invention of the printing press, the typewriter, and now the word processor, the word <u>manuscript</u> is almost anachronistic.

T F 13. The origin of <u>ambition</u> goes back to the Roman political system.

T F 14. The word <u>jest</u>, which once referred to any tale, has undergone specialization of meaning; it now means "<u>witty</u> tale."

T F 15. <u>Invaluable</u> and <u>valuable</u> are synonyms.

131

2. The following words are associated with crime, death, and punishment. Match each word with the base from which it derives.

```
___  1.  remission          A.  CID-, CIS-
___  2.  arrest             B.  DIC-, DICT-
___  3.  dissolution        C.  I-, IT-
___  4.  inquest            D.  JAC-, JECT-
___  5.  perpetrate         E.  MATR-, MATERN-
___  6.  indictment         F.  MIT(T)-, MIS(S)-
___  7.  proscription       G.  PATR-, PATERN-
___  8.  perish             H.  QUIR-, QUISIT-, QUEST-
___  9.  matron             I.  SCRIB-, SCRIPT-
___ 10.  execution          J.  SEQU-, SECUT-
___ 11.  (lethal) injection K.  SOLV-, SOLUT-
___ 12.  homicide           L.  ST(A)-, STIT-, SIST-
```

3. Indicate whether the following pairs are synonyms or antonyms by circling S or A.

```
S  A   1.  absolve       -  exonerate
S  A   2.  increase      -  reduction
S  A   3.  cogent        -  compelling
S  A   4.  subsequent    -  prior
S  A   5.  dispassionate -  biased
S  A   6.  persistent    -  tenacious
S  A   7.  register      -  roster
S  A   8.  fermentation  -  unrest
S  A   9.  proffer       -  tender
S  A  10.  itinerant     -  nomadic
S  A  11.  evolve        -  develop
S  A  12.  subjugate     -  conquer
S  A  13.  aberrant      -  normal
S  A  14.  constant      -  changeable
S  A  15.  decisive      -  inconclusive
```

4.   Supply the missing base.

1.	handwritten (text)	manu _ _ _ _ _ _
2.	lifelike	_ _ _ id
3.	unlawful	il _ _ _ al
4.	to name	_ _ _ _ _ ate
5.	to foretell	pre _ _ _ _
6.	of equal worth	equi _ _ _ ent
7.	foreknowledge	pre _ _ _ ence
8.	breakable	_ _ _ _ _ ible
9.	having a deep sound	_ _ _ orous
10.	penman	s _ _ _ _ e
11.	very small	m _ _ _ _ e
12.	growing	_ _ _ _ cent
13.	state of being alone	_ _ _ itude
14.	to withdraw from the fatherland	ex _ _ _ _ _ ate
15.	a warning	ad _ _ _ ition

5.   Word Analysis. Write the prefix (if any), base, and suffix of each word in the space provided.

		PREFIX	BASE	SUFFIX
1.	commissary	_____	_____	_____
2.	consonance	_____	_____	_____
3.	executrix	_____	_____	_____
4.	convalescence	_____	_____	_____

Part I, Review XV-XIX

		PREFIX	BASE	SUFFIX
5.	clamor			
6.	accretion			
7.	inquiry			
8.	agility			
9.	granule			
10.	vivacity			
11.	patrimony			
12.	scriptorium			
13.	monitor			
14.	conjecture			
15.	segment			
16.	minuscule			
17.	actuary			
18.	compassion			
19.	effervescence			
20.	fracture			

LESSON XX

1. Give the unshortened form of the following clipped words.

    1. brandy _____   6. mob   _____

    2. bus   _____   7. pep   _____

    3. curio   _____   8. perks   _____

    4. improv _____   9. van   _____

    5. mutt   _____   10. varsity _____

2. Circle the letter of the definition that best fits the underscored word or phrase.

    1. a derogatory remark: (A) questioning
                                  (B) disparaging
                                  (C) arrogant

    2. a precipitous cliff: (A) steep
                                  (B) rocky
                                  (C) wet

    3. in lieu of flowers: (A) in the form of
                                  (B) similar to
                                  (C) in place of

    4. a teacher's prerogative: (A) privilege
                                  (B) question
                                  (C) criticism

    5. to recapitulate the   (A) consider important
        day's events: (B) complete
                                  (C) summarize

6. couchant lions:

    (A) attacking
    (B) lying down
    (C) ravenous

7. a radical newspaper:

    (A) grass-roots
    (B) influential
    (C) advocating extreme change

8. to reconnoiter the enemy position:

    (A) attack
    (B) survey
    (C) lay siege

9. to capitalize on the situation:

    (A) take advantage of
    (B) approve of
    (C) take charge of

10. a sprightly octogenarian:

    (A) interested in ghosts
    (B) asthmatic
    (C) lively

11. to discount the story:

    (A) narrate
    (B) recollect
    (C) regard as unbelievable

12. a surrogate mother:

    (A) substitute
    (B) abusive
    (C) overly affectionate

13. to prorogue the assembly:

    (A) harangue
    (B) suspend
    (C) incite to riot

14. a certain esprit de corps:

    (A) jocosity
    (B) seductive quality
    (C) sense of unity

15. to abrogate a law:

    (A) propose
    (B) annul
    (C) denounce

In the following three exercises, match each word with the best definition.

3. LOC- *

____ 1. allocation   A. the act of moving to a new place
____ 2. collocation   B. displacement
____ 3. dislocation   C. the act of placing together
____ 4. location   D. distribution
____ 5. relocation   E. place; position

   *The verbs that correspond to these nouns end in -locate: allocate, collocate, etc.

4. SPIR- *

____ 1. aspire   A. to sweat
____ 2. conspire   B. to breathe in and out
____ 3. expire   C. to come to light
____ 4. inspire   D. to seek to attain
____ 5. perspire   E. to die
____ 6. respire   F. to plot against
____ 7. transpire   G. to breathe into: to commu-
                                   nicate by divine influence

   *The nouns that correspond to these verbs end in -(s)piration: aspiration, conspiration, etc. In addition, "conspire" has the noun-form conspiracy and "expire," expiry.

5. PUT- *

____ 1. compute   A. to accuse; to attribute something
____ 2. depute   discreditable
____ 3. dispute   B. to argue
____ 4. impute   C. to calculate
____ 5. repute   D. to consider; to deem
                             E. to appoint as an agent

   *The nouns that correspond to these verbs end in -putation: computation, deputation, etc. In addition, the verbs "dispute" and "repute" have analogous noun-forms, dispute and repute.

6. Try to supply the appropriate word from the bases introduced in Lesson XX before referring to the list of possible choices at the end of the exercise.

A. 1. A _____ is so called because of its edible root.

2. The word _____ reflects the fact that it once referred to a head covering.

3. The surface on which money is counted or business transacted is called a _____.

4. Etymologically, an officer who is "place-holding" is called a _____.

5. The person who is head of a kitchen is called a _____.

6. The etymological meaning of the verb _____ is "to prune on both sides"; its current meaning is "to remove limbs from the body."

7. Henry the VIII of England dispatched several of his wives by _____.

8. The engine that pushes or pulls a train is called a _____ because it "moves from place to place."

9. What people think about you, either good or bad, is called your _____.

10. If something has been _____, it has been "rooted out."

*   *   *

B. 1. A _____ is a vegetable that resembles the shape of a person's head.

2. The word _____ describes strong distilled liquor.

3. A woman wearing a disguise to conceal her identity is said to be _____.

4. A person who appreciates the subtleties of culture or the fine arts is called a _____.

138

5. A literary work furnished with explanatory notes is called an _____ edition.

6. An older or unmarried woman who accompanies a younger woman on a date for the sake of propriety is said to act as her _____ .

7. A large, sleeveless outer garment is called a _____ .

8. A person widely (but unfavorably) known as a result of criminal activities or outrageous behavior is termed _____ .

9. A person who is known to someone but is not a close friend is called an _____ .

10. Something that possesses an old-fashioned attractiveness or that is pleasantly odd is described as _____ .

A.	B.
amputate	acquaintance
chef	annotated
counter	cabbage
decapitation	cape
eradicated	chaperon
kerchief	connoisseur
lieutenant	incognita
locomotive	notorious
radish	quaint
reputation	spirits

7. **Review:** Indicate whether the following pairs are synonyms or antonyms by circling S or A.

S	A	1.	interjection	-	exclamation
S	A	2.	capricious	-	steadfast
S	A	3.	unconscionable	-	excessive
S	A	4.	notion	-	idea
S	A	5.	postpone	-	adjourn
S	A	6.	recount	-	narrate
S	A	7.	ambivalent	-	certain
S	A	8.	sever	-	join
S	A	9.	predominant	-	prevalent
S	A	10.	achieve	-	fail

Part I, Lesson XX

8. **Review:** Choose the correct answer by circling A or B.

    1. projectile: (A) missal   (B) missile
    2. worldly: (A) sensuous   (B) sensual
    3. to make a speech: (A) declaim   (B) disclaim
    4. stubborn: (A) perverse   (B) perverted
    5. believable: (A) credible   (B) credulous
    6. obsessive: (A) impulsive   (B) compulsive
    7. pertinent: (A) opposite   (B) apposite
    8. suggestive meaning: (A) connotation (B) denotation
    9. connective: (A) conjugal   (B) conjunctive
    10. to torment: (A) persecute   (B) prosecute

9. **Review:** The following words describe people in power, both past and present. Match each word with the base from which it derives.

    ___ 1. duchess   A. CAPIT-, (CIPIT-)
    ___ 2. count   B. CENT-
    ___ 3. regent   C. CERN-, CRET-
    ___ 4. premier   D. DECI(M)-
    ___ 5. dictator   E. DIC-, DICT-
    ___ 6. president   F. DUC-, DUCT-
    ___ 7. commissioner   G. I-, IT-
    ___ 8. secretary   H. JUR-, JUST-
    ___ 9. centurion   I. MATR-, MATERN-
    ___10. captain   J. MIT(T)-, MIS(S)-
    ___11. dean   K. PRIM-
    ___12. conquistador   L. PUT-
    ___13. deputy   M. QUIR-, QUISIT-, QUEST-
    ___14. (Supreme Court)   N. REG-, (RIG-), RECT-
            Justice   O. SED-, (SID-), SESS-
    ___15. matriarch

LESSON XXI

1. AL-, ALT-; MEDI-; MIGR-; MORT-; PET-; PUG(N)-

Match each word with the best definition.

____ 1.	exalt	A.	rival
____ 2.	prolific	B.	peevish
____ 3.	coalescence	C.	lack of ability
____ 4.	enhance	D.	an average
____ 5.	media	E.	repulsive
____ 6.	intermezzo	F.	to intensify
____ 7.	mean (n.)	G.	near death
____ 8.	transmigration	H.	request
____ 9.	emigrate	I.	productive
___10.	mortician	J.	passage of the soul into another body at death
___11.	immortal		
___12.	moribund	K.	rash
___13.	rigor mortis	L.	autopsy
___14.	impetuous	M.	blend; fusion
___15.	repeat	N.	deathless
___16.	petition	O.	rigidity of muscles after death
___17.	incompetence	P.	inclined to fight
___18.	competitor	Q.	to praise; to elevate in rank
___19.	pugnacious	R.	short musical composition between the acts of a drama
___20.	repugnant		
		S.	undertaker
		T.	to do over again
		U.	to leave one country for another
		V.	the means of communication that reach large numbers of people

2. Indicate whether each statement is true or false by circling T or F.

T F 1. Moratorium is another word for funeral home.
T F 2. The nouns medium ("one who presides at a séance") and intermediary share the idea of "acting as a go-between."
T F 3. A petulant person is one who makes a formal request.
T F 4. Mitt is a clipped form of "mitten" (MEDI-).
T F 5. A pugilist is a person who fights with the fists.
T F 6. A mezzo-soprano is a mediocre singer.

Part I, Lesson XXI

T	F	7.	Medical examiners conduct <u>post-mortem</u> examinations on victims of premature or violent deaths.
T	F	8.	The killing of one's offspring is called <u>prolicide</u>.
T	F	9.	Informally, the word <u>medieval</u> may refer to anything old-fashioned.
T	F	10.	Etymologically, an <u>altar</u> is an elevated place.
T	F	11.	<u>Hautboy</u> (ALT-) is another word for "sousaphone."
T	F	12.	The etymological meaning of <u>alumnus/alumna</u> is "foster child."
T	F	13.	The word <u>meld</u> is an example of a blend, one combining <u>melt</u> and <u>weld</u>.
T	F	14.	<u>Perpetrate</u> derives from the Latin base PET-.
T	F	15.	<u>Memento mori</u> ("remember that you must die") can refer to any reminder of death or human failings.

3. Words of Interest. Supply the appropriate word from the list below.

	Word	Etymological Meaning	Current Meaning
1.	_____	midway up the hill	ordinary
2.	_____	to put to death	to humiliate
3.	_____	a citizen contributing to the state only by producing offspring	working class
4.	_____	to fight against	to attack with words
5.	_____	a floor between floors	an intermediate story that protrudes in the form of a balcony
6.	_____	a promise to pay in the event of a person's death	the conveyance of property to a creditor
7.	_____	something that stimulates the desire to eat	a canapé, for example
8.	_____	a disease that attacks	a contagious skin disease

	Word	Etymological Meaning	Current Meaning
9.	_____	lying in the middle of land	sea situated between two continents
10.	_____	having nothing in the middle	instant; direct
11.	_____	nourishment	support paid by one spouse to the other following a divorce
12.	_____	high; lofty	snobbish; arrogant

alimony	impetus	migrant
appetizer	impugn	morbidity
haughty	mediocre	mortgage
immediate	Mediterranean	mortify
impetigo	mezzanine	proletariat

4. **Review:** Indicate whether the following pairs are synonyms or antonyms by circling S or A.

```
S  A   1.  aver          -   affirm
S  A   2.  versed        -   unfamiliar
S  A   3.  dilatory      -   prompt
S  A   4.  exquisite     -   refined
S  A   5.  predicament   -   dilemma
S  A   6.  remiss        -   conscientious
S  A   7.  refrain       -   chorus
S  A   8.  devolution    -   degeneration
S  A   9.  precipitous   -   flat
S  A  10.  provenience   -   origin
S  A  11.  adore         -   worship
S  A  12.  connoisseur   -   amateur
S  A  13.  quaint        -   ordinary
S  A  14.  cape          -   promontory
S  A  15.  incompatible  -   disagreeable
```

5. **Review:** Verb-forming suffixes. Supply the appropriate base.

1.	to make strong	_ _ _ _ ify
2.	to put in the same order	co _ _ _ _ _ ate
3.	to name	_ _ _ _ _ ate
4.	to "get in the way of": to avert	ob _ _ ate
5.	to make right	_ _ _ _ ify
6.	to pay	com _ _ _ _ ate
7.	to enlarge	_ _ _ _ ify
8.	to enlighten; to explain	e _ _ _ idate
9.	to "become strong": to recover from an illness	con _ _ _ esce
10.	to establish the truth of	_ _ _ ify
11.	to make thin; to weaken	at _ _ _ _ ate
12.	to make into one	_ _ ify
13.	to "make heavy": to worsen	ag _ _ _ _ ate
14.	to behead	de _ _ _ _ _ ate
15.	to bring to nothing; to invalidate	_ _ _ _ ify
16.	to make a god of	_ _ ify
17.	to put to death on a cross	_ _ _ _ ify
18.	to make light; to relieve	al _ _ _ iate
19.	to question formally	inter _ _ _ ate
20.	to make sacred	con _ _ _ _ ate

LESSON XXII

1. Use a check to indicate which of the following pairs are doublets.

____	1.	confuse	-	confound
____	2.	compound	-	complicate
____	3.	cruise	-	cross
____	4.	matron	-	patron
____	5.	motif	-	motion
____	6.	deceased	-	departed
____	7.	imply	-	implicate
____	8.	regal	-	kingly
____	9.	recapitulation	-	precipitous
____	10.	impetus	-	impetigo

2. <u>GRAT-; MISC-, MIXT-; NEG-; PURG-; VULG-</u>

   Match each word with the best definition.

____ 1. disgrace	A.	slender
____ 2. gracile	B.	to declare publicly
____ 3. congratulate	C.	indiscriminate
____ 4. grace	D.	to cleanse; to eliminate
____ 5. ingratiate	E.	self-denial
____ 6. gratuity	F.	to gain the favor of others
____ 7. agreeable	G.	to honor; to adorn
____ 8. medley	H.	a tip
____ 9. mixture	I.	dishonor
____ 10. promiscuous	J.	to be ungrateful
____ 11. denial	K.	anything having two or more
____ 12. abnegation		diverse elements
____ 13. negate	L.	assertion that something is false
____ 14. purge	M.	to express joy over someone's
____ 15. promulgate		achievement
	N.	congenial
	O.	to nullify
	P.	lacking elegance
	Q.	musical "mixture" of passages
		taken from other compositions

3. MOV-, MOT-

    Supply the appropriate word from the list below.

    1. cinema   _____

    2. recurrent movement or theme   _____

    3. not movable; fixed   _____

    4. a lowering in rank   _____

    5. elevation in rank   _____

    6. to disband   _____

    7. an instant of time   _____

    8. disturbance; confusion   _____

    9. movable   _____

    10. incentive   _____

    11. self-propelled vehicle   _____

    12. a strong, subjective feeling   _____

    13. far removed; secluded   _____

    14. rebellion   _____

    15. impetus behind a crime
        or action   _____

automobile	immobile	motive
commotion	mobile	movies
demobilize	moment	mutiny
demotion	motif	promotion
emotion	motivation	remote

Part I, Lesson XXII

4. Words of Interest. Supply the appropriate word from the list
   below.

	Word	Etymological Meaning	Current Meaning
1.	_____	purely blind	obtuse
2.	_____	common	crude
3.	_____	gratitude	elegance of motion
4.	_____	to deny again	to go back on a promise
5.	_____	to make known to the people	to disclose
6.	_____	mixed-mixed	in a hasty or con-fused manner
7.	_____	renouncer of the faith	traitor
8.	_____	mixed	a person of mixed blood
9.	_____	purified; strained	a cooked and sieved food
10.	_____	the changeable common people	a disorderly or lawless crowd

divulge	miscegenation	purée
grace	mob	renegade
melee	pell-mell	renege
mestizo	purblind	vulgar

5. Indicate whether each statement is true or false by circling T
   or F.

T F 1. Most authors are delighted when school administrators
           expurgate passages from their literary works.
T F 2. Purgatory is a place where one's sins are cleansed.
T F 3. A person who performs a service gratis expects a big
           tip.

147

T F   4. <u>Vulgarism</u> and the <u>Vulgate</u> (the Latin translation of the
           Bible) share the same base.
T F   5. <u>Miscellanea</u> and <u>potpourri</u> are synonyms.
T F   6. A <u>natatorium</u> is a nursery for newborns.
T F   7. The etymological meaning of <u>meddle</u> is "to mix" into
           someone else's business.
T F   8. A <u>doublet</u> refers to two or more words in the same
           language that enter by different routes of transmission
           from the same source.
T F   9. If someone serves a dish called a <u>medley</u>, it contains a
           mélange of ingredients.
T F 10. <u>Mustang</u> ultimately derives from the Latin base MISC-,
           MIXT-.

6. **Review:** Choose the correct answer by circling A or B.

     1. incapable of being
         solved: (A) insolvent   (B) insoluble

     2. to misrepresent: (A) contort   (B) distort

     3. truthful: (A) veracious   (B) voracious

     4. inflicting extreme
         pain: (A) torturous   (B) tortuous

     5. to deduce: (A) infer   (B) imply

     6. graphic: (A) vivacious   (B) vivid

     7. to examine: (A) prove   (B) probe

     8. to supply with
         light: (A) elucidate   (B) illuminate

     9. authorized: (A) official   (B) officious

    10. a direction to
         a pharmacist: (A) proscription (B) prescription

11. aware: (A) conscientious (B) conscious

12. enunciation: (A) diction   (B) dictation

13. an ornament: (A) pensive   (B) pendant

14. petulant: (A) fractious   (B) fractional

15. slight: (A) negligible   (B) negligent

16. urgent: (A) exigent   (B) exiguous

17. easily broken: (A) fragile   (B) fractious

18. to accuse: (A) indict   (B) indite

19. inventive: (A) ingenuous   (B) ingenious

20. prudent: (A) judicious   (B) judicial

21. incentive: (A) motive   (B) motif

22. bury: (A) inter   (B) enter

23. ornate: (A) flagrant   (B) flamboyant

24. something that
     attracts: (A) magnet   (B) magnate

25. injurious: (A) noxious   (B) obnoxious

26. to kiss: (A) osculate   (B) oscillate

27. manner: (A) mode   (B) mold

28. biased: (A) tenuous   (B) tendentious

29. skeptical: (A) incredible   (B) incredulous

30. artificial: (A) factious   (B) factitious

7. **Review:** In the following two exercises, circle the bases and then match each word with the best definition.

___ 1.	insidious	A.	contributive
___ 2.	verbal	B.	to inform
___ 3.	conducive	C.	expressed orally
___ 4.	initiate	D.	ambition
___ 5.	dissolute	E.	to discontinue a session
___ 6.	congested	F.	treacherous
___ 7.	aspiration	G.	loose in morals
___ 8.	notify	H.	disgraceful
___ 9.	ignominious	I.	overcrowded
___10.	prorogue	J.	to commence

*   *   *

___ 1.	allocation	A.	indigenous
___ 2.	mortally	B.	fringe benefit
___ 3.	extract (n.)	C.	deviation
___ 4.	mediocre	D.	a letter
___ 5.	missive	E.	laborious study
___ 6.	aberration	F.	fatally
___ 7.	lucubration	G.	average
___ 8.	migratory	H.	nomadic
___ 9.	perquisite	I.	distribution
___10.	native	J.	excerpt; quotation

LESSON XXIII

1. <u>PORT-</u> *

   Match each word with the best definition.

___ 1. comportment	A.	expulsion from a country
___ 2. deportation	B.	a detailed account of news
___ 3. exportation	C.	conduct; bearing
___ 4. importation	D.	act of furnishing evidence for
___ 5. purport		or providing livelihood to
___ 6. reportage	E.	act of bringing in goods from a
___ 7. support		foreign country for sale or trade
___ 8. transport	F.	rapture; ecstasy
	G.	an apparent purpose; significance
	H.	act of sending goods abroad for
		sale or trade

   *The verbs that correspond to these nouns end in -port:
   <u>comport</u>, <u>deport</u>, etc.

2. Indicate whether the following pairs are synonyms or antonyms
   by circling S or A.

S	A	1.	deflect	–	deviate
S	A	2.	import	–	insignificance
S	A	3.	convince	–	persuade
S	A	4.	invincible	–	insurmountable
S	A	5.	indeterminate	–	definite
S	A	6.	destroy	–	exterminate
S	A	7.	manifest	–	abstruse
S	A	8.	mandatory	–	compulsory
S	A	9.	flexible	–	rigid
S	A	10.	demand	–	require
S	A	11.	rapport	–	affinity
S	A	12.	importunate	–	urgent
S	A	13.	vanquish	–	defeat
S	A	14.	terminate	–	initiate
S	A	15.	reflective	–	pensive

3. Words of Interest. Supply the appropriate word from the list below.

Word	Etymological Meaning	Current Meaning
1. _____	little hand	handcuff
2. _____	sliding gate	iron grating in a medieval castle that prevents passage
3. _____	harbor	a sweet, red wine
4. _____	a handful of men	shrewd management for one's own interests
5. _____	to release from slavery	to liberate
6. _____	blowing toward the harbor	favorable
7. _____	cloak-carrier	large leather suitcase
8. _____	to conquer completely	to demonstrate clearly
9. _____	to operate by hand	to work toward a pre-determined goal
10. _____	something struck by the hand	public declaration of intentions
11. _____	harmony	a portable musical instrument
12. _____	animal accustomed to the hand	a large dog
13. _____	end; boundary	a word peculiar to a specific group or activity
14. _____	of the hand	customary way of acting
15. _____	to mark off the boundaries	to decide

accordion manifesto porch
determine manikin port
emancipate manipulation portcullis
evince manner porter
manacle mastiff portmanteau
maneuver opportune term

4. STRU-, STRUCT-

Supply the appropriate word from the list below.

1. directions _____

2. any part of a building
above the foundations _____

3. total devastation _____

4. the supporting part of a
building _____

5. to build _____

6. tool _____

7. diligent; assiduous _____

8. to interpret; to explain _____

9. hindrance _____

10. promoting improvement _____

construct destruction obstruction
constructive industrious reconstruction
construe instructions substructure
destroy instrument superstructure

5.   Indicate whether each statement is true or false by circling T
     or F.

T   F   1. Someone who is <u>portly</u> carries a lot of weight.
T   F   2. <u>Amanuensis</u> and <u>manicurist</u> are synonymous terms.
T   F   3. <u>Vincent</u> is an appropriate name for a man keen on
            winning.
T   F   4. The etymological meaning of <u>portfolio</u> is "a carrier for
            leaves (of paper)."
T   F   5. A <u>portmanteau word</u> is restricted to terms and
            expressions having to do with travel.
T   F   6. <u>Sport</u> is a clipped form of "disport."
T   F   7. In some schools, students are graded on their
            <u>deportment</u>.
T   F   8. <u>Genuflection</u> is an example of a reflex action.
T   F   9. The act of <u>manumission</u> dates back to the time of the
            ancient Romans.
T   F 10. The verbal suffix -fy means "to make."

6. <u>CORD-</u>

    Match each word with the best definition.

____ 1. courage   A. to dishearten
____ 2. cordial   B. consonant
____ 3. encourage   C. support on a hinged church seat
____ 4. discourage   D. to hearten
____ 5. discordant   E. valor
____ 6. accordant   F. harmony
____ 7. record (n.)   G. inconsonant
____ 8. core   H. the best performance documented
____ 9. concord   I. friendly
____ 10. misericord   J. the heart of the matter

Part I, Lesson XXIII

7. **Review:** Circle the letter of the word in each group that does not mean the same as the others.

1. (A) decimate
    (B) extort
    (C) exterminate
    (D) eradicate

2. (A) reputation
    (B) renown
    (C) infamy
    (D) fame

3. (A) inconsequential
    (B) trivial
    (C) incontinent
    (D) negligible

4. (A) achieve
    (B) attain
    (C) accomplish
    (D) aver

5. (A) sequential
    (B) extraordinary
    (C) noteworthy
    (D) exceptional

6. (A) submit
    (B) succumb
    (C) decapitate
    (D) capitulate

7. (A) disclaim
    (B) subscribe
    (C) disavow
    (D) repudiate

8. (A) composite
    (B) reproduction
    (C) ditto
    (D) replica

9. (A) rejoinder
    (B) retort
    (C) reply
    (D) repose

10. (A) discountenance
    (B) depredation
    (C) deprecation
    (D) disapproval

11. (A) confirm
    (B) prove
    (C) confound
    (D) substantiate

12. (A) apposite
    (B) relevant
    (C) inconstant
    (D) pertinent

13. (A) dispassionate
    (B) equitable
    (C) objective
    (D) indigent

14. (A) vindicate
    (B) justify
    (C) pursue
    (D) support

15. (A) contort
    (B) efface
    (C) expunge
    (D) remove

16. (A) diary
    (B) journal
    (C) descant
    (D) record

155

8. **Review:** Clothing. Match each word with the base from which it derives.

____	1.	vest	A. CAPIT-, (CIPIT-)
____	2.	lingerie	B. CORPOR-, CORP(US)-
____	3.	miniskirt	C. DU-
____	4.	apparel	D. FORT-
____	5.	suit	E. LEG-, (LIG-), LECT-
____	6.	negligee	F. LINE-
____	7.	cape	G. MEDI-
____	8.	dress	H. MINOR-, MINUS-, MINUT-
____	9.	doublet	I. PAR-
____	10.	corset	J. PEND-, PENS-
____	11.	suspenders	K. REG-, (RIG-), RECT-
____	12.	comforter	L. SEQU-, SECUT-
____	13.	visor	M. UMBR- ("shade")
____	14.	mittens	N. VEST-
____	15.	sombrero	O. VID-, VIS-

9. **Review:** Business. Match each word with its <u>etymological</u> meaning.

____	1.	depository	A. terms drawn up
____	2.	affluent	B. to argue over a set of ten hides
____	3.	dicker	C. job without care
____	4.	amortize	D. a person who believes or trusts
____	5.	firm	E. overflowing (with wealth)
____	6.	sinecure	F. (money) that comes back
____	7.	deficit	G. a fixed business
____	8.	creditor	H. to make one
____	9.	manager	I. it is lacking
____	10.	revenue	J. sum or share to be divided
____	11.	contract	K. place for money to be set aside
____	12.	corporation	L. horse trainer
____	13.	dividend	M. free from debt
____	14.	unionize	N. a body
____	15.	solvent	O. to extinguish a debt

LESSON XXIV

1. Indicate whether the following pairs are synonyms or antonyms by circling S or A.

```
S  A   1.  enunciation      -  diction
S  A   2.  denounce         -  acclaim
S  A   3.  satiety          -  deficiency
S  A   4.  disobedient      -  compliant
S  A   5.  impressive       -  awesome
S  A   6.  renounce         -  disclaim
S  A   7.  impressionable   -  naïve
S  A   8.  satisfied        -  discontented
S  A   9.  announce         -  promulgate
S  A  10.  appropriate      -  unseemly
S  A  11.  audition         -  tryout
S  A  12.  obeisance        -  homage
S  A  13.  propriety        -  indecorum
S  A  14.  pressure         -  stress
S  A  15.  saturate         -  drench
```

2. <u>PRESS-</u>

   Match each word with the best definition.*

```
___  1.  compress        A.  to indicate one's feelings
___  2.  depress             or opinions
___  3.  express         B.  to condense
___  4.  impress         C.  to subject someone to harsh
___  5.  oppress             authority
___  6.  repress         D.  to quell a rebellion
___  7.  suppress        E.  to discourage; to sadden
                         F.  to influence favorably
                         G.  to hold back feelings in
                             the subconscious
```

   *The nouns that correspond to these verbs end in -press or -pression: <u>compress</u>, <u>compression</u>, <u>depression</u>, etc.

3. Words of Interest. Supply the appropriate word from the list below.

1. to heed   _____

2. a literary genre   _____

3. messenger to the Pope   _____

4. media   _____

5. unhappy   _____

6. a traveling amusement show   _____

7. formal examination of rec-
    ords to check their accuracy   _____

8. lit. one's own: a piece of
    land   _____

9. a withered old woman   _____

10. entire property subject to
    payment of debts   _____

11. to rebuke severely   _____

12. a flesh-colored flower   _____

assets	crone	property
audit	nuncio	reprimand
carnation	obey	sad
carnival	press	satire

4. Review: Circle the letter of the best definition.

1. to <u>mince</u> words: (A) moderate (B) mumble (C) misuse

2. a <u>tortuous</u> route: (A) painful (B) winding (C) hidden

3. a <u>patronizing</u> attitude: (A) condescending (B) fatherly
    (C) typical of one's ancestors

4. terminal cancer: (A) located in the extremities
(B) operable (C) causing death

5. to portage a canoe: (A) paddle (B) approach the dock
from the left (C) carry over land from one body of water
to another

6. adverse weather: (A) hostile (B) favorable (C) fickle

7. an incumbent candidate: (A) presently holding office
(B) unlikely to win (C) likely to win

8. an illuminated manuscript: (A) medieval (B) ahead of its
time (C) decorated with elaborate illustrations

9. casualties of war: (A) people lost (B) catalepts
(C) horrors

10. a perfidious friend: (A) faithful to a fault (B) long-
time (C) disloyal

11. Yankee ingenuity: (A) naïveté (B) inventiveness
(C) rapacity

12. aberrant behavior: (A) deviant (B) transient
(C) conforming

13. tenuous evidence: (A) insubstantial (B) convincing
(C) massive

14. plaited hair: (A) braided (B) thick (C) dyed

15. a semiannual event: occurring (A) every other year
(B) yearly (C) twice a year

16. specious reasoning: (A) deceptive (B) capacious
(C) logical

17. a magnanimous gesture: (A) cowardly (B) noble
(C) emotional

18. malicious gossip: (A) false (B) spiteful
(C) unjustified

19. nefarious deeds: (A) varied (B) numerous (C) evil

20. a commuted prison sentence: (A) exchanged for one less
severe (B) lengthened (C) unreasonably severe

21. impending disaster: (A) natural (B) unfortunate
     (C) imminent

22. to lead a sedentary life: (A) characterized by sitting
     (B) rebellious (C) nomadic

23. a provocative book: (A) obscene (B) stimulating
     (C) revealing

24. an auspicious occasion: (A) suggestive (B) propitious
     (C) unhappy

25. workmen's compensation: (A) occupational hazard
     (B) dues, as to a union (C) payment for injury

5. **Review:** Animals. Match each word with the base(s) from which
    it derives.

___ 1.	terrier	A.	ANIM-
___ 2.	insect	B.	CANT-, (CENT-), [CHANT-]
___ 3.	animalcule	C.	CAPIT-, (CIPIT-)
___ 4.	salmon	D.	CENT-
___ 5.	osprey	E.	CUMB-, CUB-
___ 6.	praying mantis	F.	DOM(IN)-
___ 7.	cattle	G.	FLAG(R)-, FLAM(M)-
___ 8.	stallion	H.	FRANG-, (FRING-), FRACT-
___ 9.	centipede	I.	MAN(U)-
___10.	mastiff	J.	MIGR-
___11.	chanticleer	K.	PED-
___12.	flamingo	L.	PREC-
___13.	covey	M.	SAL-, (SIL-),
___14.	dam		SALT-, (SULT-)
___15.	migratory (birds)	N.	SEC-, SEG-, SECT-
		O.	ST(A)-, STIT-, SIST-
		P.	TERR-

LESSON XXV

1. Give the plural(s) of each of the following nouns.

    1. alumna   _____

    2. alumnus   _____

    3. atrium   _____

    4. corpus   _____

    5. crux   _____

    6. datum   _____

    7. index   _____

    8. medium   _____

    9. rabies   _____

    10. stimulus   _____

2. Match each word with the best definition.

___	1. opprobrium	A.	gap
___	2. quorum	B.	customs; habits
___	3. impetus	C.	as
___	4. interim	D.	a majority
___	5. mores	E.	boredom
___	6. lacuna	F.	beyond what is seen or said
___	7. qua	G.	momentum
___	8. tedium	H.	disgrace
___	9. ulterior	I.	burden
___	10. onus	J.	interval

3. The following words are Latin verbs. Give their current English meanings. (Note that in English these words are nouns.)

Latin Word	Translation	English Meaning
1. caret	there is lacking	_____
2. caveat	let him/her beware	_____
3. credo	I believe	_____
4. deficit	it is wanting	_____
5. fiat	let it be done	_____
6. ignoramus	we do not know	_____
7. imprimatur	let it be printed	_____
8. lavabo	I shall wash	_____
9. memento	remember	_____
10. placebo	I shall please	_____
11. tenet	he/she holds	_____
12. affidavit	he/she has sworn	_____

4. Match each word with the best definition.

___ 1.	quondam	A.	judge
___ 2.	requiem	B.	former
___ 3.	quasi	C.	a likeness
___ 4.	odium	D.	panacea
___ 5.	ergo	E.	hatred
___ 6.	simulacrum	F.	a very poor person
___ 7.	consortium	G.	dirge
___ 8.	nostrum	H.	therefore
___ 9.	arbiter	I.	resembling
___ 10.	pauper	J.	a large financial partnership

5. Words of Interest. Supply the appropriate word from the list below.

	Latin Word	Translation	English Meaning
1.	_____	shepherd	clergyman
2.	_____	on the left side	ominous; malevolent
3.	_____	sandy place	enclosed area used for spectator sports
4.	_____	hearth	center of attention
5.	_____	manly woman	strong woman; shrew
6.	_____	almost-island	Florida, for example
7.	_____	little rod	rod-shaped bacterium
8.	_____	do everything	person employed to do many different things
9.	_____	madness	infectious disease that affects the nervous system
10.	_____	a yawning	a gap; a lapse
11.	_____	threads of life spun by the Fates	endurance
12.	_____	Our Father. . .	Lord's Prayer
13.	_____	make similar	replica
14.	_____	mask; character	the character one assumes
15.	_____	spark	trace

arena	hiatus	rabies
bacillus	pastor	scintilla
facsimile	Paternoster	sinister
factotum	peninsula	stamina
focus	persona	virago

6. Indicate whether the following pairs are synonyms or antonyms by circling S or A.

```
S  A   1.  gratis       -   costly
S  A   2.  dictum       -   pronouncement
S  A   3.  apex         -   vertex
S  A   4.  omen         -   portent
S  A   5.  acumen       -   dullness
S  A   6.  ardor        -   indifference
S  A   7.  effluvium    -   miasma
S  A   8.  vertigo      -   equilibrium
S  A   9.  proviso      -   stipulation
S  A  10.  finis        -   commencement
```

7. Match each phrase with the best definition.

```
____  1.  status quo          A.  something indispensable
____  2.  magnum opus         B.  to the point of nausea
____  3.  in situ             C.  conversely
____  4.  sine qua non        D.  a great work
____  5.  pro forma           E.  one of a kind; unique
____  6.  sui generis         F.  in the original position
____  7.  ad nauseam          G.  deductive
____  8.  ne plus ultra       H.  existing state of affairs
____  9.  vice versa          I.  carried out as a formality
____ 10.  a priori            J.  the highest point
```

8. Match each phrase with the best definition.

```
____  1.  in extremis         A.  intrinsically
____  2.  casus belli         B.  unwelcome person
____  3.  quid pro quo        C.  stiffening of the body
____  4.  per se                  after death
____  5.  in toto             D.  with great distinction
____  6.  ad hoc              E.  in the place of a parent
____  7.  rigor mortis        F.  near death
____  8.  in loco parentis    G.  totally
____  9.  persona non grata   H.  something given or taken
____ 10.  magna cum laude         for something else
                             I.  for a particular purpose
                             J.  justification or stimulus
                                 for war
```

9. Give the meanings of the following Latin abbreviations.

1. A.D.   (<u>anno</u> <u>Domini</u>)

2. a.m.   (<u>ante</u> <u>meridiem</u>)

3. c.   (<u>circa</u>)

4. cf.   (<u>confer</u>)

5. e.g.   (<u>exempli</u> <u>gratia</u>)

6. et al.   (<u>et</u> <u>alia</u>)

7. etc.   (<u>et</u> <u>cetera</u>)

8. ibid.   (<u>ibidem</u>)

9. i.e.   (<u>id</u> <u>est</u>)

10. loc. cit.   (<u>loco</u> <u>citato</u>)

11. N.B.   (<u>nota</u> <u>bene</u>)

12. op. cit.   (<u>opere</u> <u>citato</u>)

13. Q.E.D.   (<u>quod</u> <u>erat</u> <u>demonstrandum</u>)

14. seq.   (<u>sequente</u>)

15. vs.   (<u>versus</u>)

10. Expressions of Interest. Supply the appropriate phrase from the list below.

Latin Phrase	Translation	English Meaning
1. _____	in good faith	genuine; sincere
2. _____	rare bird	unusual person
3. _____	body of the crime	physical evidence of a crime
4. _____	another "I"	a second self
5. _____	into the middle of things	in the middle of a narrative
6. _____	in glass	in a test tube
7. _____	one out of many	slogan of the U.S.
8. _____	my fault	formal acknowledgment of personal fault
9. _____	while the crime is blazing	in the act; red-handed
10. _____	voice of the people	popular opinion
11. _____	under the rose	secretly
12. _____	at one's pleasure	to improvise
13. _____	not of sound mind	mentally incompetent
14. _____	nourishing mother	school from which one has graduated
15. _____	to the man	appealing to emotions rather than intellect

ad hominem	corpus delicti	non compos mentis
ad-lib	e pluribus unum	non sequitur
(ad libitum)	flagrante delicto	per capita
alma mater	in medias res	rara avis
alter ego	in vitro	sub rosa
bona fide	mea culpa	vox populi

REVIEW OF LESSONS XX-XXV

1. Give the unshortened form of the following clipped words.

   1. ad _____   4. memo _____

   2. auto _____   5. sport _____

   3. blitz _____   6. still _____

2. Circle the letter of the word that best fits the definition.

   1. to condemn:
      (A) announce
      (B) denounce
      (C) renounce

   2. to appropriate:
      (A) abrogate
      (B) arrogate
      (C) derogate

   3. to amuse oneself:
      (A) comport
      (B) deport
      (C) disport

   4. to accelerate:
      (A) capitulate
      (B) precipitate
      (C) recapitulate

   5. a striving to attain:
      (A) aspiration
      (B) inspiration
      (C) transpiration

   6. enlightening:
      (A) constructive
      (B) destructive
      (C) instructive

   7. to argue:
      (A) compute
      (B) depute
      (C) dispute

   8. unearned:
      (A) gratuitous
      (B) ingrate
      (C) ingratiating

3. Supply the appropriate word from the list below.

1. a list of corrections _____

2. our (home) remedy _____

3. a list of things to be done _____

4. with deference to _____

5. lit. let it be printed _____

6. by way of _____

7. something that serves as a reminder _____

8. a biological category _____

9. feeling of hostility _____

10. small, insignificant details _____

11. a demon in female form believed to lie with men _____

12. propriety _____

13. the end _____

14. something made like another; a copy _____

15. lit. I believe _____

agenda   facsimile   minutiae
animus   finis   nostrum
corrigenda   genus   pace
credo   imprimatur   succubus
decorum   memento   via

4. Indicate whether each statement is true or false by circling T
   or F.

T F   1. A product bearing the notice caveat emptor is likely to
          be endorsed by a consumer group.
T F   2. Loco ("crazy") derives from the Latin base LOC-.
T F   3. A man with an extraordinarily inflated opinion of
          himself is said to have an alter ego.
T F   4. If a criminal is caught in flagrante delicto, chances
          are "the jig is up."
T F   5. The expression "if you scratch my back, I'll scratch
          yours" is roughly equivalent to the Latin quid pro quo.
T F   6. A defendant's plea of nolo contendere in a criminal
          proceeding is equivalent to an admission of guilt.
T F   7. Originally, quaint meant "knowledgeable" or "clever."
T F   8. A man who marries a virago can look forward to many
          years of domestic harmony and connubial bliss.
T F   9. The words sad and sadist are etymologically related.
T F 10. In a story beginning in medias res, the author starts
          the narrative in the middle of the sequence of events.
T F 11. The unshortened form of piano is "pianoforte."
T F 12. If someone appears unexpectedly to resolve a
          particularly difficult situation, that person may be
          described as a deus ex machina.
T F 13. Caret is a Latin word used by jewelers to indicate the
          weight of precious stones.
T F 14. A detective who speaks of a criminal's M.O. is
          referring to the culprit's modus operandi.
T F 15. The etymological meaning of satire--a genre the Romans
          claimed to have invented--is "medley."

5. Circle the letter of the correct plural(s) of each word.

   1. lacuna: (A) lacunas   (B) lacunae   (C) lacunes

   2. matrix: (A) matrixa   (B) matrixii   (C) matrices

   3. colloquium: (A) colloquies (B) colloquia (C) colloquiae

   4. nucleus: (A) nucleuses (B) nuclea   (C) nuclei

   5. appendix: (A) appendixae (B) appendices (C) appendixes

169

6. Match each word with the best definition.

___ 1. rapport   A. a mark made by pressure
___ 2. convict (n.)   B. a severe reproof
___ 3. mixture   C. correct behavior
___ 4. carnage   D. a seasonal movement
___ 5. imprint   E. blend
___ 6. vulgar   F. bellicose
___ 7. proprietor   G. crude
___ 8. moment   H. a person found guilty of
___ 9. reprimand   committing a crime
___10. evince   I. to cleanse
___11. terminal (adj.)   J. delay
___12. pugnacious   K. a harmonius relation
___13. migration   L. an instant of time
___14. purge   M. massive slaughter
___15. destructive   N. final
                                            O. to show clearly
                                            P. ruinous
                                            Q. owner

7. Supply the missing base.

1. deathless   im _ _ _ _ al

2. a critical hearing   _ _ _ ition

3. thankfulness   _ _ _ _ itude

4. a seeking   _ _ _ ition

5. to root out   e _ _ _ _ _ ate

6. heartfelt; gracious   _ _ _ _ ial

7. to place   _ _ _ ate

8. the middle   _ _ _ _ an

9. by hand   _ _ _ _ al

10. to behead   de _ _ _ _ _ ate

11. to bend   f _ _ _

12. to sweat   per _ _ _ e

13. height   _ _ _ itude

14. lack of knowledge   i _ _ _ rance

15. middleman   inter _ _ _ _ ary

8. The French Connection. Match each word with the base from which it derives.

____ 1. mischief   A. AL-, ALT-
____ 2. lieu   B. AUD-
____ 3. recount   C. CAPIT-, (CIPIT-)
____ 4. charnel   D. CARN-
____ 5. sprightly   E. CORD-
____ 6. meddle   F. GRAT-
____ 7. construe   G. LOC-
____ 8. haughty   H. MAN(U)-
____ 9. courage   I. MISC-, MIXT-
____10. obey   J. MORT-
____11. agreeable   K. MOV-, MOT-
____12. mortgage   L. NUNCI-
____13. manner   M. PUT-
____14. announcement   N. SPIR-
____15. motif   O. STRU-, STRUCT-

9. Match each phrase with the best definition.

____ 1. ad hoc   A. the necessary changes having been made
____ 2. cui bono   B. at first sight
____ 3. modus vivendi   C. solid ground
____ 4. mutatis mutandis   D. manner of living
____ 5. non sequitur   E. voice of the people: popular opinion
____ 6. post scriptum   F. it doesn't follow
____ 7. prima facie   G. for whose good; for whose benefit
____ 8. status quo   H. the existing state of affairs
____ 9. terra firma   I. something written afterwards
____10. vox populi   J. for this only

LATIN REVIEW

1. Indicate whether each statement is true or false by circling T or F.

T F   1. <u>Dismal</u> is made up of the prefix dis- and the base MAL-.
T F   2. A <u>verbicide</u> is guilty of wanton destruction of the English language.
T F   3. The guillotine is a device that effects death by <u>recapitulation</u>.
T F   4. A <u>sciolist</u> is "one who knows little," a possessor of superficial knowledge.
T F   5. <u>Sui generis</u> and <u>rara avis</u> both can refer to people or things that are unique.
T F   6. "Antidisestablishmentarianism" qualifies as <u>sesquipedalian</u>.
T F   7. The etymology of <u>nasturtium</u> is "nasty-smelling" flower.
T F   8. A person who dresses <u>ostentatiously</u> dresses in an understated fashion.
T F   9. The etymology of <u>penultimate</u> is "nearly last."
T F 10. Originally, a <u>nomenclator</u> was a slave who accompanied his master in order to tell him the names of people he met when campaigning for office.
T F 11. <u>A.D.</u> and <u>B.C.</u> are both Latin abbreviations.
T F 12. The prefix in- means the same in <u>ingratiate</u> and <u>ingrate</u>.
T F 13. <u>Dirigible</u> derives from the Latin base REG-, (RIG-), RECT-.
T F 14. The Latin <u>sinister</u> and the French <u>gauche</u>, words originally referring to the left, have undergone degeneration of meaning.
T F 15. <u>Pro forma</u> and the informal <u>rubber stamp</u> are equivalent in meaning.

2. Supply the missing base.

1. pertaining to sight   _ _ _ ual

2. concerning nutrition   _ _ imentary

3. underground   sub _ _ _ _ anean

4. handwritten (text)   _ _ _ _ script

5. to restore to the
    fatherland   re _ _ _ _ _ ate

6. changeable   _ _ _ able

7. to write carelessly   _ _ _ _ _ ble

8. manifold   _ _ _ _ iple

9. meat eating   _ _ _ _ ivorous

10. thousand-year period   _ _ _ _ ennium

11. incapable of being heard   in _ _ _ ible

12. a place   _ _ _ ale

13. pertaining to the end   _ _ _ al

14. farewell address   vale _ _ _ _ ion

15. lover   _ _ orist

16. between the lines   inter _ _ _ _ ar

17. one who fights with
    the fists   _ _ _ ilist

18. evil-doer   _ _ _ _ factor

19. to think   _ _ _ itate

20. cinema   _ _ _ ies

Part I, Review

3. Form the antonym of each word by substituting another prefix. Remember assimilation.

1. dissonance   _____ sonance

2. increase   _____ crease

3. antebellum   _____ bellum

4. encourage   _____ courage

5. deficient   _____ ficient

6. destructive   _____ structive

7. demotion   _____ motion

8. import   _____ port

9. proponent   _____ ponent

10. ingest   _____ gest

4. Circle the letter of the definition that best fits the underscored word.

1. a boon companion: (A) lachrymose (B) faithful (C) convivial

2. gratuitous violence: (A) unwarranted (B) graphic (C) censored

3. a restaurant's ambience: (A) cuisine (B) atmosphere (C) service

4. conjugal relations: (A) strained (B) amiable (C) between husband and wife

5. illegible handwriting: (A) easily deciphered (B) unreadable (C) cursive

6. prenatal care: (A) postpartum (B) before birth (C) pertaining to delivery

7. an infraction of the rules: (A) violation (B) exception (C) a small portion

175

8. to <u>avail</u> <u>oneself</u> <u>of</u> a service: (A) pay for (B) reject
   (C) make use of

9. <u>abject</u> poverty: (A) moderate (B) utterly hopeless
   (C) abandoned

10. a <u>persistent</u> salesman: (A) pertinacious (B) successful
    (C) traveling

11. a <u>voluble</u> personality: (A) talkative (B) explosive
    (C) worthy

12. to <u>discount</u> a theory: (A) originate (B) disregard
    (C) discuss

13. a <u>sullen</u> child: (A) undernourished (B) only (C) surly

14. <u>extenuating</u> circumstances: (A) mitigating (B) embar-
    rassing (C) relaxing

15. a <u>derogatory</u> remark: (A) inquiring (B) disparaging
    (C) complimentary

16. <u>mortal</u> wounds: (A) fatal (B) traumatic (C) corporal

17. a <u>prolific</u> writer: (A) published (B) suffering from
    writer's block (C) productive

18. to <u>divulge</u> a secret: (A) embellish (B) reveal
    (C) maintain

19. to <u>flex</u> one's muscles: (A) relax (B) build (C) bend

20. <u>constructive</u> criticism: (A) helpful (B) unsolicited
    (C) adverse

21. an <u>expurgated</u> version of a book: (A) unabridged
    (B) bowdlerized (C) condensed

22. a <u>viable</u> alternative: (A) workable (B) long-lived
    (C) preferable

23. the <u>advent</u> of spring: (A) harbinger (B) end (C) arrival

24. a <u>compendious</u> comparison: (A) verbose (B) concise
    (C) grotesque

25. a <u>discursive</u> style: (A) digressive (B) flowing
    (C) severe

5. Occupations. Match each word with the base from which it derives.

___	1. artisan	A.	AG-, (IG-), ACT-
___	2. infantryman	B.	ART-
___	3. bus (driver)	C.	CRUC-
___	4. actuary	D.	FA(B), FAT-, FESS-, FAM-
___	5. announcer	E.	FER-
___	6. crusader	F.	LOQU-, LOCUT-
___	7. obstetrician	G.	MIS(S)-, MIT(T)-
___	8. exterminator	H.	NOV-
___	9. referee	I.	NUNCI-, [NOUNC-]
___	10. printer	J.	OMN-
___	11. ventriloquist	K.	PRESS-
___	12. bartender	L.	SEQU-, SECUT-
___	13. novelist	M.	ST(A)-, STIT-, SIST-
___	14. emissary	N.	TEND-, TENT-, TENS-
___	15. prosecutor	O.	TERMIN-

6. Indicate which are clipped words by placing a check next to them.

___ 1. flu   ___ 3. punctilio
___ 2. motel   ___ 4. decaf

Indicate which pairs are doublets by placing a check next to them.

___ 1. afflatus-flaunt   ___ 3. count-compute
___ 2. exclude-foreclose   ___ 4. flora-fluorite

Indicate which words have undergone elevation of meaning by placing a check next to them.

___ 1. constable   ___ 3. pioneer
___ 2. amateur   ___ 4. nice

Indicate which words have undergone degeneration of meaning by placing a check next to them.

___ 1. plausible   ___ 3. prestige
___ 2. wench   ___ 4. villain

7. Match each word with its <u>etymological</u> meaning.

    ___ 1.   mustang   A. blazing
    ___ 2.   recantation   B. we do not know
    ___ 3.   flagrant   C. a singing back
    ___ 4.   corpuscle   D. nourishing mother
    ___ 5.   ignoramus   E. to kill every tenth man
    ___ 6.   senator   F. elder
    ___ 7.   spectator   G. cross-dresser
    ___ 8.   pomegranate   H. little body
    ___ 9.   expunge   I. a turning as one
    ___10.   decimate   J. to mark out with dots
    ___11.   ignominious   K. teacher
    ___12.   alma mater   L. mixed breed
    ___13.   universe   M. having no name
    ___14.   transvestite   N. seedy apple
    ___15.   doctor   O. one who watches

8. Match each word with the best definition.

    ___ 1.   appropriateness   A. to perplex
    ___ 2.   abstruse   B. circumspect
    ___ 3.   compatible   C. exoneration
    ___ 4.   probation   D. to plot
    ___ 5.   torture   E. difficult to understand
    ___ 6.   extempore   F. the rhythm of events
    ___ 7.   confuse   G. request
    ___ 8.   residence   H. to inflict pain
    ___ 9.   cadence   I. conditional release
    ___10.   contagious   J. congruent
    ___11.   conspire   K. capable
    ___12.   able   L. suitability
    ___13.   absolution   M. impromptu
    ___14.   discreet   N. infectious
    ___15.   petition   O. domicile

9. Indicate whether the following pairs are synonyms or antonyms by circling S or A.

    S A   1. acrimonious   -   stinging
    S A   2. animated   -   vivacious
    S A   3. divinity   -   immortal
    S A   4. educated   -   illiterate
    S A   5. affirm   -   deny
    S A   6. affluent   -   impecunious
    S A   7. fallacious   -   veracious
    S A   8. gregarious   -   introverted
    S A   9. precarious   -   dangerous
    S A 10. levity   -   gravity
    S A 11. ordinary   -   mediocre
    S A 12. alien   -   extraterrestrial
    S A 13. model   -   pattern
    S A 14. retreat   -   recede
    S A 15. elate   -   enrapture
    S A 16. injurious   -   noxious
    S A 17. strict   -   lenient
    S A 18. plenteous   -   abundant
    S A 19. conservative -   radical
    S A 20. inquisitive   -   curious

10. Indicate which words have been affected by folk etymology by placing a check next to them.

    ___ 1. female   ___ 3. crayfish
    ___ 2. pencil   ___ 4. reindeer

    Indicate which words are blends by placing a check next to them.

    ___ 1. brunch   ___ 3. NATO
    ___ 2. rebus   ___ 4. buzz

    Indicate which words are diminutives by placing a check next to them.

    ___ 1. scruple   ___ 3. minuet
    ___ 2. senile   ___ 4. oracle

11. Circle the prefixes (if any) and bases and give their
    meanings; then indicate whether each word is a noun, an
    adjective, or a verb by circling N, A, or V.

MEANINGS

1.	abundant	_____	N A V
2.	apartment	_____	N A V
3.	aquarium	_____	N A V
4.	circumference	_____	N A V
5.	corrigendum	_____	N A V
6.	defamation	_____	N A V
7.	effervesce	_____	N A V
8.	endurance	_____	N A V
9.	executrix	_____	N A V
10.	extrasensory	_____	N A V
11.	immigrate	_____	N A V
12.	latitude	_____	N A V
13.	lectern	_____	N A V
14.	pertinacious	_____	N A V
15.	precursor	_____	N A V
16.	rapid	_____	N A V
17.	salient	_____	N A V
18.	superfluity	_____	N A V
19.	turbulent	_____	N A V
20.	verify	_____	N A V

PART II

WORD ELEMENTS FROM GREEK

THE GREEK ALPHABET

Form	Name	Transliteration
A α	alpha	a
B β	beta	b
Γ γ	gamma	g
Δ δ	delta	d
E ε	epsilon	e
Z ζ	zeta	z
H η	eta	e
Θ ϑ	theta	th
I ι	iota	i
K κ	kappa	k, c
Λ λ	lambda	l
M μ	mu	m
N ν	nu	n
Ξ ξ	xi	x
O o	omicron	o
Π π	pi	p
P ρ	rho	r, rh
Σ ς, σ	sigma	s
T τ	tau	t
Y υ	upsilon	u, y
Φ φ	phi	ph
X χ	chi	ch
Ψ ψ	psi	ps
Ω ω	omega	o

Give the current meanings of the following words that derive from the names of the Greek letters.

1. alpha

2. alphabet

3. chiasmus

4. Chi-Rho

5. delta

6. gamut

7. iota (cf. jot)

8. lambdacism

9. omega

10. sigmoid

LESSONS I & II

1. In the following two exercises, match each word or phrase with
    the best definition.

____	1. amazon	A.	extremely fanciful
____	2. Procrustean	B.	gloomy
____	3. chimerical	C.	wise counselor
____	4. nemesis	D.	to tease
____	5. stygian	E.	a very wealthy man
____	6. halcyon	F.	strong, powerful woman
____	7. mentor	G.	calm; peaceful
____	8. labyrinth	H.	retribution; unbeatable opponent
____	9. tantalize	I.	a long wandering
____	10. odyssey	J.	point of vulnerability
____	11. aegis	K.	maze
____	12. Achilles' heel	L.	effecting conformity by violent means
		M.	extremely changeable
		N.	protection or sponsorship

*   *   *

____	1. laconic	A.	permanently threatening danger
____	2. sword of Damocles	B.	person of discriminating taste, esp. in food and wine
____	3. philippic	C.	person devoted to luxury
____	4. Draconian	D.	sun worshiper
____	5. solecism	E.	stinging condemnation
____	6. epicure	F.	pertaining to a victory won at great cost
____	7. cynic	G.	person devoted to house pets, especially dogs
____	8. sybarite	H.	grammatical or social error
____	9. ostracism	I.	person who believes all human actions are prompted by self-interest
____	10. Pyrrhic	J.	extremely harsh
		K.	concise
		L.	exclusion from society

2. **Optional Latin Review:** Choose the word or phrase from the list below that fits each expression <u>etymologically</u>.

1. "I could simply die"   _____

2. the heart of the matter   _____

3. "Go with God"   _____

4. having the rear end in front   _____

5. a spiritual flock   _____

6. "If you scratch my back,
    I'll scratch yours"   _____

7. person with whom you break
    bread   _____

8. little mouse   _____

9. a going off the furrow   _____

10. caught while the crime
    is blazing   _____

11. person clad in white   _____

12. moonstruck   _____

13. eater of hashish   _____

14. to harrow again   _____

15. "Give him a hand"   _____

adieu	congregation	mortified
assassin	core	muscle
candidate	delirium	preposterous
commend	flagrante delicto	quid pro quo
companion	lunatic	rehearse

LESSON III

In the following three exercises, match each word with the best
definition.

1. OD-

____ 1. epode	A. emotional utterance; ecstasy; musical improvisation
____ 2. tragedy	B. a singing back: recantation
____ 3. monody	C. concert hall
____ 4. odeum	D. short lyric poem
____ 5. comedy	E. tune; song
____ 6. rhapsody	F. goat song: tale of disaster
____ 7. parody	G. burlesque imitation
____ 8. palinode	H. mirth song: drama with a happy ending
____ 9. melody	I. song sung by one voice
____ 10. ode	J. song sung after another song: third part of a Greek ode

2. BIBLI-; CRYPT-, CRYPH-; TOM-

____ 1. bibliomania	A. typical or ideal example
____ 2. bibliotheca	B. smallest part of an element
____ 3. Bible	C. secret; obscure
____ 4. bibliography	D. any large, scholarly book
____ 5. bibliophile	E. of doubtful authorship
____ 6. cryptic	F. extreme preoccupation with collecting books
____ 7. grotesque	G. booklover: collector of books
____ 8. apocryphal	H. having a secret name
____ 9. cryptonymous	I. a list of references
____ 10. dichotomy	J. excision of a breast
____ 11. epitome	K. collection of books
____ 12. tome	L. division, esp. of two mutually exclusive groups
____ 13. mastectomy	M. distorted in appearance
____ 14. atom	N. study of insects
____ 15. entomology	O. the "Good Book"

3. CANON-; CYCL-; GLOSS-, GLOT(T)-; ICON-; MIM-; PYR-

____ 1. canonical
____ 2. bicycle
____ 3. cyclone
____ 4. encyclopedia
____ 5. glossal
____ 6. gloss
____ 7. polyglot
____ 8. iconoclast
____ 9. iconology
____10. mimic
____11. mimeograph
____12. pyromaniac
____13. pyrosis
____14. empyrean
____15. pyroclastic

A. pertaining to the tongue
B. study of artistic symbolism
C. conforming to a general rule
D. heartburn
E. multilingual
F. a work that contains information on all branches of knowledge
G. an expert on religious representations
H. attacker of established beliefs
I. heavens
J. note of explanation
K. to make copies on a stencil
L. a violent storm characterized by circular wind motion
M. involving volcanic action
N. to imitate
O. two-wheeler
P. pertaining to fire fighting
Q. person with a passion for setting fires

4. **Review:** Words from Greek Mythology, History, and Philosophy. Choose the appropriate word from the list below.

1. Race of female warriors   _____

2. Beautiful youth who fell in love with his own image   _____

3. King who wished that everything he touched would turn to gold   _____

4. Structure built to house the Minotaur   _____

5. Protagonist of a Greek tragedy
    who killed his father and
    married his mother   _____

6. Place in Greece proverbial for
    its pastoral way of life   _____

7. Greeks known for rigid self-
    discipline   _____

8. Sea nymphs whose enticing songs
    lured men to their deaths   _____

9. River proverbial for its winding
    course   _____

10. Tomb of Mausolus   _____

11. Mythical highwayman whose bed was
    "one size fits all"   _____

12. Codifier of extremely severe laws _____

13. Monster with the head of a lion,
    the body of a goat, and the tail
    of a serpent   _____

14. Shield of Zeus and later Athena _____

15. Famous cynic in search of an
    honest man   _____

aegis	Draco	Narcissus
Amazons	labyrinth	Oedipus
Arcadia	Mausoleum	Procrustes
Chimera	Meander	Sirens
Diogenes	Midas	Spartans

5. Optional Latin Review: Indicate whether the following pairs are synonyms or antonyms by circling S or A.

S	A	1.	aberrant	-	deviant
S	A	2.	approve	-	sanction
S	A	3.	ordinary	-	mediocre
S	A	4.	supererogatory	-	necessary
S	A	5.	impulse	-	incentive
S	A	6.	subjoin	-	append
S	A	7.	supposition	-	assumption
S	A	8.	indiscreet	-	circumspect
S	A	9.	divert	-	distract
S	A	10.	aggrieved	-	distressed
S	A	11.	animated	-	inert
S	A	12.	appropriate	-	arrogate
S	A	13.	integrity	-	unity
S	A	14.	modern	-	antiquated
S	A	15.	reclamation	-	recovery

6. Optional Latin Review: Indicate whether each statement is true or false by circling T or F.

T F 1. Cluster derives from the Latin base CLUD-, CLUS-.
T F 2. The pronunciation of purblind closely reflects its current meaning, "purely blind," hence "obtuse."
T F 3. Still is a clipped form of "distillery."
T F 4. Corduroy derives from the Latin base CORD-.
T F 5. Duplicity and exploit are doublets.
T F 6. The etymology of partake is to "take part."
T F 7. Flu is a clipped form of "influenza."
T F 8. A portmanteau word is the same thing as a blend.
T F 9. Ambiance is an incorrect spelling of ambience.
T F 10. A somniloquist is a sleep-talker; a somnambulist is a sleepwalker.

LESSON IV

1. ALG-

   Match each word with the best definition.

___ 1.	pantalgia	A.	headache
___ 2.	nostalgia	B.	pain all over
___ 3.	cephalgia	C.	sensitivity to pain
___ 4.	neuralgia	D.	foot pain
___ 5.	podalgia	E.	fear of pain
___ 6.	odontalgia	F.	pain-producing
___ 7.	algesia	G.	nerve pain
___ 8.	algogenic	H.	"homesickness": a longing for things past
___ 9.	analgesic	I.	toothache
___10.	algophobia	J.	painkiller

2. Circle the prefixes and bases and then give the meaning of each element.

		PREFIX	BASE
1.	dialectic	_____	_____
2.	anachronism	_____	_____
3.	catalyst	_____	_____
4.	apogee	_____	_____
5.	atrophy	_____	_____
6.	antipodal	_____	_____
7.	catalogue	_____	_____
8.	apotheosize	_____	_____
9.	catholic	_____	_____
10.	amphibious	_____	_____

191

3. Indicate whether each statement is true or false by circling T
    or F.

T   F   1. The word <u>pandemonium</u> etymologically corresponds to the
             modern expression "all hell breaking loose."
T   F   2. An atheist would strongly favor the establishment of a
             <u>theocracy</u>.
T   F   3. A <u>pyrotechnist</u> is in particular demand on the fourth of
             July.
T   F   4. A <u>pandemic</u> disease is confined to a small area.
T   F   5. <u>Eumenides</u> ("Well-minded Ones") is another name for the
             Greek Furies.
T   F   6. If someone is <u>chronically</u> late, the tardiness is
             habitual.
T   F   7. A person who has an extreme fear of surgical operations
             should avoid physicians who are <u>tomomaniacs</u>.
T   F   8. A <u>threnody</u> is performed on festive occasions.
T   F   9. In Greek mythology, the prophecies of <u>Cassandra</u> were
             always heeded and always came true.
T   F   10. <u>Panacea</u> and <u>nostrum</u> are synonyms.
T   F   11. <u>Melodious</u> and <u>odious</u> derive from the same Greek base.
T   F   12. A <u>biblioclast</u> is a person who defaces library books.
T   F   13. <u>Grotto</u> ultimately derives from the Greek base CRYPT-.
T   F   14. <u>Apocrypha</u> are writings of certain authenticity.
T   F   15. According to some etymologists, <u>crony</u> ("chum") derives
             from the Greek base CHRON-.

4. <u>LOG-</u>, [<u>LOGUE-</u>]

    Match each word with the best definition.

____ 1. logical   A. concluding section
____ 2. analogy   B. excessive wordiness
____ 3. apology   C. the symbol "&," for example
____ 4. dialogue   D. reasonable
____ 5. logorrhea   E. uncomplimentary
____ 6. epilogue   F. a group of three plays or
____ 7. eulogistic   literary works
____ 8. dyslogistic   G. expression of regret
____ 9. trilogy   H. a "gathering up" for comparison
____ 10. logogram   I. conversation
                            J. flattering

192

5. __BI-; GE-; MNE-; POD-; THE-; TROPH-__

Match each word with the best definition.

___ 1.	biotic	A.	belief in many gods
___ 2.	biography	B.	all the gods of a particular
___ 3.	geometry		people
___ 4.	amnesia	C.	passionate ("having a god within")
___ 5.	amnesty	D.	an official forgetting:
___ 6.	mnemonics		a general pardon
___ 7.	hypermnesia	E.	origin of the gods
___ 8.	tripod	F.	speaker's platform
___ 9.	podium	G.	loss of memory
___10.	atheism	H.	belief in one God
___11.	monotheism	I.	an exceptionally poor memory
___12.	theogony	J.	branch of science dealing with
___13.	enthusiastic		measurement
___14.	pantheon	K.	relating to life
___15.	hypertrophy	L.	art of improving the memory
		M.	belief in no gods
		N.	an exceptionally excellent memory
		O.	the story of a person's life
		P.	excessive growth
		Q.	three-legged stool

6. __Review:__ Match each word with the best definition.

___ 1.	prologue	A.	alimentary
___ 2.	pantophagous	B.	annals
___ 3.	anthology	C.	contemporaneous
___ 4.	chronicles	D.	florilegium
___ 5.	analysis	E.	multilingual
___ 6.	eclogue	F.	omnivorous
___ 7.	polyglot	G.	preface
___ 8.	synchronous	H.	resolution
___ 9.	monologue	I.	literary selection
___10.	trophic	J.	soliloquy

7. **Review:** Supply the missing prefix or base.

    1. with feet opposite

        anti _ _ _ al

    2. capable of life on
        both land and water

        _ _ _ _ _ bious

    3. person who believes
        in many gods

        poly _ _ _ ist

    4. without nourishment

        _ trophy

    5. the study of life

        _ _ ology

    6. something back in
        (or out of) time

        _ _ _ chronistic

    7. speaking one language

        mono _ _ _ _

    8. fear of pain

        _ _ _ ophobia

    9. to imitate

        _ _ _ ic

    10. person with a passion
        for setting fires

        _ _ _ omaniac

8. **Optional Latin Review:** Circle the letter of the word that best
    fits the definition.

    1. endless:

        (A) determinant
        (B) exterminate
        (C) indeterminate
        (D) interminable

    2. to prove guilty:

        (A) convict
        (B) convince
        (C) evict
        (D) evince

    3. onerous:

        (A) expressive
        (B) impressive
        (C) oppressive
        (D) repressive

4. to grant:

    (A) accord
    (B) concord
    (C) discord
    (D) record

5. condemnation:

    (A) denunciation
    (B) enunciation
    (C) pronunciation
    (D) renunciation

6. apathetic:

    (A) dispassionate
    (B) impassioned
    (C) impassive
    (D) passionate

7. anatomy:

    (A) bisection
    (B) dissection
    (C) intersection
    (D) resection

8. to narrate:

    (A) account
    (B) count
    (C) discount
    (D) recount

9. to summarize:

    (A) capitulate
    (B) decapitate
    (C) precipitate
    (D) recapitulate

10. apathy:

    (A) indifference
    (B) inference
    (C) preference
    (D) sufferance

11. poverty:

    (A) constitution
    (B) destitution
    (C) institution
    (D) substitution

12. epigraph:

    (A) ascription
    (B) inscription
    (C) prescription
    (D) subscription

13. to free:

    (A) intermit
    (B) manumit
    (C) remit
    (D) submit

14. to vanquish:

    (A) compress
    (B) depress
    (C) express
    (D) suppress

15. immediate:

    (A) constant
    (B) distant
    (C) extant
    (D) instant

16. enunciation:

    (A) addiction
    (B) condition
    (C) diction
    (D) interdiction

17. to make into law:

    (A) enact
    (B) exact
    (C) interact
    (D) transact

18. bellicose:

    (A) fractious
    (B) fragile
    (C) frail
    (D) refractory

19. harmony:

    (A) assonance
    (B) consonance
    (C) dissonance
    (D) resonance

20. to renounce:

    (A) abjure
    (B) adjure
    (C) conjure
    (D) perjure

LESSON V

1. Circle the prefixes and bases and then give the meaning of each element.

		PREFIX	BASE
1.	dystrophy	_____	_____
2.	eclogue	_____	_____
3.	ectoderm	_____	_____
4.	empyreal	_____	_____
5.	encyclical	_____	_____
6.	endogamy	_____	_____
7.	ephemeral	_____	_____
8.	epigeous	_____	_____
9.	eudemonic	_____	_____
10.	exodus	_____	_____

2. <u>CENTR-</u>

Match each word with the best definition.

____ 1. concentric
____ 2. eccentric
____ 3. egocentric
____ 4. monocentric
____ 5. theocentric
____ 6. androcentric
____ 7. ethnocentric
____ 8. heliocentric
____ 9. geocentric
____ 10. anthropocentric

A. regarding one's own group as center
B. single-centered
C. regarding the sun as center
D. off-center: peculiar; odd
E. regarding mankind as center
F. having a common center
G. regarding God as center
H. regarding the self as center
I. regarding the earth as center
J. regarding males or masculine interests as center

3. Words of Interest.   Supply the appropriate word from the list below.

	Word	Etymological Meaning	Current Meaning
1.	_____	empty tomb	monument for person whose body is buried elsewhere
2.	_____	pillar used by ancient Greeks as a gravestone	inscribed stone slab used for commemorative purposes
3.	_____	person sent out	any person who initiates reform
4.	_____	first combatant	leading character in a literary work
5.	_____	something written on a tomb	inscription on a tomb
6.	_____	easy death	mercy killing
7.	_____	for one day only	short-lived
8.	_____	leader of the people	a person who gains power by playing on people's emotions
9.	_____	a meeting	a church council
10.	_____	messenger	a messenger of God
11.	_____	lacking blood	lacking vigor or creativity
12.	_____	message (= a sending to)	a letter, especially a formal one
13.	_____	contest	dramatic conflict among characters in a literary work
14.	_____	Greek garment	woman's scarf or fur
15.	_____	messenger of good news	a preacher of the gospel

agon	demagogue	evangelist
anemic	democrat	leukemia
angel	ephemeral	protagonist
angelophany	epistle	stele
apostle	epitaph	stole
cenotaph	euthanasia	synod

4. AGON-; ANGEL-; DEM-; HEM(AT)-, HAEM(AT)-; OD-, HOD-; STOL-, STAL-, STLE-; THANAT-, THANAS-

Match each word with the best definition.

____ 1.	antagonize	A.	affecting many people
____ 2.	Los Angeles	B.	a component of red blood cells
____ 3.	epidemic	C.	instrument for measuring distance traveled
____ 4.	endemic		
____ 5.	hemoglobin	D.	interval
____ 6.	hemorrhage	E.	native
____ 7.	hemophiliac	F.	heavy bleeding
____ 8.	odometer	G.	city of angels
____ 9.	exodus	H.	waves of contraction in the digestive system
____ 10.	methodical		
____ 11.	period	I.	emigration
____ 12.	episode	J.	to oppose
____ 13.	epistolary	K.	obituary
____ 14.	peristalsis	L.	a view of death
____ 15.	thanatopsis	M.	"bleeder"
		N.	catatonic
		O.	of or pertaining to letters
		P.	systematic
		Q.	event

5. <u>GAM-</u>

Supply the appropriate word from the list below.

1. If you marry a second time, that marriage is called
   _____.

2. If you marry a person while still legally married to
   another, you are guilty of _____.

3. If you believe in marrying outside of a specific group,
   you practice _____.

4. If you marry into an equal or higher social group, you are
   practicing _____.

5. If you think a person should have one spouse at a time,
   you believe in _____.

6. If you have several spouses at the same time, you are a
   _____.

7. If you marry for the third time, you enter into
   _____.

8. If you hate the thought of marriage, you are a
   _____.

bigamy	exogamy	monogamy
digamy	hypergamy	polygamist
endogamy	misogamist	trigamy

6. Indicate whether each statement is true or false by circling T
or F.

T F 1. <u>Panic</u>, all-encompassing fear, derives from the Greek
          base PAN(T)-.
T F 2. Someone who faints at the sight of blood is <u>hemophobic</u>.
T F 3. If you practice <u>allogamy</u>, you are probably a plant.
T F 4. In some states homicide is punishable by
          <u>electrothanasia</u>.

T F 5. <u>Taps</u>, the bugle call played at military funerals, derives from the Greek base TAPH-.

T F 6. As its title suggests, Boccaccio's <u>Decameron</u> contains ten days of storytelling.

T F 7. William Harvey was a pioneer in the study of <u>hemodynamics</u>.

T F 8. <u>Iconoclast</u> enters the English language through the world of art; the word originally referred to a careless sculptor.

T F 9. A census provides the government with <u>demographic</u> information.

T F 10. A person suffering from <u>thanatophobia</u> should avoid precarious situations.

T F 11. Henry VIII of England was famous for <u>gamomania</u>.

T F 12. A <u>Pyrrhic</u> victory is one in which the conquered succumb as a result of total conflagration.

T F 13. <u>Cenobitic</u> and <u>sybaritic</u> are similar in meaning.

T F 14. <u>Pantheon</u> may refer to a group of luminaries in a particular field.

T F 15. A <u>monoglot</u> has facility in several languages.

7. **Review:** Match each word with the best definition.

___ 1.	trophic	A.	anguish
___ 2.	polytheism	B.	lingual
___ 3.	podiatrist	C.	tip of the tongue
___ 4.	panoply	D.	heat-producing
___ 5.	meteorology	E.	a complete array
___ 6.	anatomy	F.	insensitivity to pain
___ 7.	pyrogenetic	G.	a structure that covers the glottis during swallowing
___ 8.	epiglottis		
___ 9.	cyclic	H.	changeable
___ 10.	crypt	I.	not occurring at the same time
___ 11.	agony	J.	belief in more than one god
___ 12.	glossal	K.	recurring regularly in succession
___ 13.	analgesia	L.	science of climate and weather
___ 14.	octopus	M.	foot doctor
___ 15.	asynchronous	N.	nutritional
		O.	a subterranean burial chamber
		P.	science dealing with the structure of organisms
		Q.	eight-footed mollusk

8. **Optional Latin Review:** Indicate whether each statement is true or false by circling T or F.

T F 1. According to some etymologists, <u>parasol</u> and <u>umbrella</u> derive from the same Latin base.

T F 2. <u>Funambulist</u> is another word for "tightrope walker."

T F 3. <u>Quentin</u> is a particularly appropriate name for a fourth child of the male gender.

T F 4. <u>Mold</u> ("fungus") derives from the Latin base MOD-.

T F 5. <u>Reverberate</u> belongs to the VERB- family of words.

T F 6. The word <u>money</u> derives from the Roman goddess of finances, Juno Moneta.

T F 7. Body parts and functions often are sources for euphemisms.

T F 8. <u>Capitol</u> derives from the Latin <u>capitolium</u> (< CAPIT-), a chief temple of Jupiter at Rome.

T F 9. The etymology of <u>garner</u> is "to collect grains."

T F 10. <u>Prescience</u> is a prerequisite for a job as a fortune teller.

LESSON VI

1. <u>ONYM-</u>

   Match each word with its example.

   ___ 1. acronym   A. Venus (for love)

   ___ 2. antonym   B. Mark Twain

   ___ 3. eponym   C. sow (a pig)--sow (to scatter seed)

   ___ 4. heteronym   D. buzz or choo-choo

   ___ 5. homonym   E. heal--health

   ___ 6. metonymy   F. Johnson

   ___ 7. onomatopoeia   G. Death Valley

   ___ 8. paronym   H. NATO

   ___ 9. patronymic   I. fortitude--strength

   ___10. pseudonym   J. bear (to carry)--bear (an animal)

   ___11. synonym   K. Americus Vespucius

   ___12. toponym   L. day--night

2. Circle the prefixes and bases and then give the meaning of each element.

		PREFIX	BASE
1.	hyperpyrexia	_____	_____
2.	hyperglycemia	_____	_____
3.	hypogeal	_____	_____
4.	metamorphose	_____	_____

Part II, Lesson VI

<table>
<thead>
<tr><th></th><th>PREFIX</th><th>BASE</th></tr>
</thead>
<tbody>
<tr><td>5. metaphor</td><td></td><td></td></tr>
<tr><td>6. paralyze</td><td></td><td></td></tr>
<tr><td>7. parody</td><td></td><td></td></tr>
<tr><td>8. period</td><td></td><td></td></tr>
<tr><td>9. periphery</td><td></td><td></td></tr>
<tr><td>10. problem</td><td></td><td></td></tr>
<tr><td>11. prognosticate</td><td></td><td></td></tr>
<tr><td>12. prologue</td><td></td><td></td></tr>
<tr><td>13. prosody</td><td></td><td></td></tr>
<tr><td>14. symbol</td><td></td><td></td></tr>
<tr><td>15. syntax</td><td></td><td></td></tr>
</tbody>
</table>

3. Indicate whether each statement is true or false by circling T or F.

T F 1. A common pachyderm, among the more exotic elephant, hippopotamus, and rhinoceros, is the domestic bore.

T F 2. That the etymology of nun is believed by some to be "mother" or "wet-nurse" is an example of a paradox.

T F 3. Ball (a lavish party) and the ball in baseball both derive from the Greek base BALL-.

T F 4. Know is unrelated to the Greek base GNO(S)-.

T F 5. Pyrophoric material is nonflammable.

T F 6. The etymological meaning of devil is "slanderer."

T F 7. Dermabrasion is sometimes recommended for the removal of acne scars.

T F 8. Gnothi seauton (Greek for "know thyself") is an example of an aphorism.

T F 9. The word paraphernalia originally referred to the personal belongings of a Greek soldier.

T F 10. Couples having difficulty choosing a name for their new baby may consult an onomasticon.

204

4. **BALL-, BOL-, BLE-**

   The French Connection. The words in this exercise have
   entered English through French. They ultimately derive from
   the Greek base BALL-, BOL-, BLE-. Match each with the best
   definition.

   ____ 1. ballet   A. simple, often sentimental song
   ____ 2. parlor   B. idle talk
   ____ 3. ballad   C. conditional release from prison
   ____ 4. palaver   D. allegorical story
   ____ 5. parliament   E. a room suitable for conversation
   ____ 6. parlance   F. discussion; informal conference
   ____ 7. parable   to discuss peace terms
   ____ 8. parley   G. any legislative body
   ____ 9. parole   H. manner of speaking
                           I. a classical dance form

5. Circle the letter of the correct definition.

   1. <u>homily</u>: (A) grits (B) sermon (C) ugly

   2. <u>semaphore</u>: (A) system of visual signaling (B) diesel
      trailer (C) microorganism

   3. <u>metabolic</u>: (A) ecstatic (B) figurative (C) undergoing
      change

   4. <u>mesomorphic</u>: (A) a muscular physique (B) a heavy body
      build (C) a slight physique

   5. <u>hyperbolic</u>: (A) fiendish (B) defeated (C) exaggerated

   6. <u>physiognomy</u>: (A) the face, esp. as an index of character
      (B) physical geography (C) system of physical laws

   7. <u>dogmatic</u>: (A) canine (B) tenacious (C) doctrinaire

   8. <u>emblem</u>: (A) representation (B) profit (C) secret code

   9. <u>gnomic</u>: (A) troll-like (B) characterized by aphorism
      (C) pertaining to knowledge

   10. <u>orthodox</u>: (A) theological (B) educational (C) con-
       ventional

11. homogeneous: (A) having the same nature (B) having the same parent (C) having the same name

12. tactics: (A) diplomacy (B) science of touch (C) strategy

13. amphora: (A) a two-handled vase (B) insignia (C) entrails

14. morphology: (A) physical fitness (B) study of structure or form (C) study of body types

15. anonymous: (A) in complete agreement (B) lively (C) of unknown name

16. gnostic: (A) atheistic (B) knowing (C) playful

17. taxidermy: (A) a levy on animal pelts (B) irritation of the skin (C) the art of stuffing and mounting animals in lifelike form

18. ballistics: (A) science of training professional dancers (B) study of the motion of projectiles (C) study of the healthful effects of bathing

19. diabolic: (A) overthrown (B) devilish **(C) hot as the devil**

20. metaphor: (A) a figure of speech (B) a system of signals (C) a striking change

6. **Review:** Words from Greek Mythology, History, and Philosophy. Choose the appropriate word from the list below.

1. Dark; gloomy _____

2. A permanently threatening danger _____

3. Exclusion from a group _____

4. A collection of maps _____

5. Clever but fallacious reasoning _____

6. An evil that cannot be
   removed by one attempt   _____

7. The Fate who assigned
   one's destiny   _____

8. A small but vulnerable
   weakness   _____

9. Person who doubts the sin-
   cerity of human actions   _____

10. A learned society   _____

academy	Clotho	sophistry
Achilles' heel	hydra	stygian
atlas	Lachesis	sword of
cynic	ostracism	Damocles

7. **Review:** Literary Terms. Match each word with the best
   definition.

____ 1. eclogues
____ 2. rhapsodist
____ 3. trilogy
____ 4. georgic
____ 5. mimesis
____ 6. episode
____ 7. onomatopoeia
____ 8. protagonist
____ 9. cycle
____10. symbol

A. formation of words whose sounds
   suggest the meaning
B. a poem dealing with farming
C. an object that represents something
   else through association
D. series of three dramas
E. epic singer in ancient Greece
F. leading actor in a drama
G. series of poems dealing with a
   single theme or hero
H. a section of an ancient Greek
   tragedy between two choric songs
I. imitation of nature
J. poetry in which shepherds converse

8.　Review:　Supply the appropriate synonym from the list below.

1.　glossal　＿＿＿＿＿＿＿＿＿＿＿＿

2.　periphery　＿＿＿＿＿＿＿＿＿＿＿＿

3.　polymorphous　＿＿＿＿＿＿＿＿＿＿＿＿

4.　anamnesis　＿＿＿＿＿＿＿＿＿＿＿＿

5.　entomophagous　＿＿＿＿＿＿＿＿＿＿＿＿

6.　anonymous　＿＿＿＿＿＿＿＿＿＿＿＿

7.　dogma　＿＿＿＿＿＿＿＿＿＿＿＿

8.　prognostication　＿＿＿＿＿＿＿＿＿＿＿＿

9.　palinode　＿＿＿＿＿＿＿＿＿＿＿＿

10.　onomastic　＿＿＿＿＿＿＿＿＿＿＿＿

11.　demotic　＿＿＿＿＿＿＿＿＿＿＿＿

12.　athanasia　＿＿＿＿＿＿＿＿＿＿＿＿

13.　metamorphose　＿＿＿＿＿＿＿＿＿＿＿＿

14.　hypogeal　＿＿＿＿＿＿＿＿＿＿＿＿

15.　exodus　＿＿＿＿＿＿＿＿＿＿＿＿

circumference	insectivorous	prescience
doctrine	lingual	recantation
emigration	multiform	recollection
immortality	nominal	subterranean
innominate	popular	transform

REVIEW OF LESSONS I-VI

1. Form the <u>antonym</u> of each word by changing its prefix.

		Antonym	Meaning of Antonym
1.	antonym:	_____	_____
2.	endoderm:	_____	_____
3.	dysphoria:	_____	_____
4.	hypertrophy:	_____	_____
5.	ectomorph:	_____	_____
6.	dyslogistic:	_____	_____
7.	hypoglycemia:	_____	_____
8.	anode:	_____	_____
9.	eutrophy:	_____	_____
10.	katabasis:	_____	_____

2. Indicate whether the following pairs are synonyms or antonyms by circling S or A.

S	A	1.	Protean	-	rigid
S	A	2.	angelic	-	demonic
S	A	3.	agonizing	-	excruciating
S	A	4.	chronic	-	acute
S	A	5.	labyrinth	-	maze
S	A	6.	orthodox	-	unconventional
S	A	7.	anemic	-	vigorous
S	A	8.	apocryphal	-	genuine
S	A	9.	empyreal	-	celestial
S	A	10.	gnome	-	aphorism
S	A	11.	siren	-	seductive
S	A	12.	pandemic	-	universal
S	A	13.	laconic	-	pithy
S	A	14.	anomaly	-	consistency
S	A	15.	epicure	-	gourmand

3. Words of Interest.   Supply the appropriate word from the list below.

	Word	Etymological Meaning	Current Meaning
1.	_____	foot-trap	gout
2.	_____	a forgetting	a general pardon
3.	_____	a longing for a return home	a longing for things past
4.	_____	the abode of all demons	utter chaos or disorder
5.	_____	things hidden	works of doubtful authorship
6.	_____	a singing back	retraction
7.	_____	a throwing beyond	exaggeration
8.	_____	cure-all	a remedy for all diseases
9.	_____	a piece cut off	a large, learned book
10.	_____	a bride's goods beyond her dowry	personal belongings
11.	_____	breaker of images	person who attacks established beliefs
12.	_____	wicker basket	small container for food items
13.	_____	state of having a god within	intense excitement
14.	_____	goat song	tale of disaster
15.	_____	government by the people	rule by the majority

agnostic	enthusiasm	pandemonium
amnesty	hyperbole	Pandora
apocrypha	iconoclast	paraphernalia
canister	nostalgia	podagra
demagoguery	palinode	tome
democracy	panacea	tragedy

4. Match each prefix with its meaning.

```
___  1.  apo-        A.  through; across; between
___  2.  dia-        B.  around; near
___  3.  en-         C.  not; without
___  4.  epi-        D.  from; off
___  5.  para-       E.  in; into
___  6.  peri-       F.  both; on both sides of
                     G.  beside; disordered
                     H.  upon; to; in addition to
```

5. Indicate whether each statement is true or false by circling T or F.

T F   1. Bigamy and digamy are considered synonymous in current usage.

T F   2. A prognosticator puts off until tomorrow what he or she could be doing today.

T F   3. Dogmatic and canine are synonyms.

T F   4. Hype is a clipped form of hypodermic.

T F   5. Tax and taxi both derive from the Greek base TACT-, TAX-.

T F   6. A frequent complaint among senior citizens is that they suffer from hypermnesia.

T F   7. The etymological meaning of grotesque is "characteristic of a grotto."

T F   8. Canapé ultimately derives from the Greek base CANON-.

T F   9. The etymological meaning of anthology is "a selection of flowers."

T F 10. A woman whose clothes, coiffure, and make-up reflect a fashion in vogue twenty years ago may be described as anachronistic.

6. Circle the bases and then match each word with the best definition.

____	1. panorama	A.	collection of books
____	2. systole	B.	a concluding section
____	3. cryptonym	C.	loss of sensation due to injury or disease
____	4. bibliotheca		
____	5. diagnose	D.	to examine for the purpose of determining a disease
____	6. pyre	E.	to imitate
____	7. paralysis	F.	comprehensive survey
____	8. epitaph	G.	"Round-eye"
____	9. Cyclops	H.	diametrically opposite
____	10. epilogue	I.	empty tomb
____	11. gloss	J.	secret name
____	12. mimic (v.)	K.	one of the three Fates
____	13. atrophy	L.	the living together of two unlike organisms
____	14. symbiosis		
____	15. antipodal	M.	inscription on a tomb
		N.	a wasting away as a result of malnutrition
		O.	a note of explanation
		P.	rhythmic contraction of the heart
		Q.	pile of combustible material for burning a dead body

LESSON VII

1. AESTHE-, ESTHE-; ANTHROP-; ARCHA(E)-, ARCHE-; GEN(E)-, GON-;
    GER(ONT)-; HOL-; PEP(T)-

    Match each word with the best definition.

___ 1.	esthesis	A.	pertaining to old age
___ 2.	telesthesia	B.	mental telepathy
___ 3.	anthropocentric	C.	Gabriel, for example
___ 4.	archetype	D.	expanse of water with many
___ 5.	archangel		scattered islands
___ 6.	archipelago	E.	gloomy
___ 7.	archenemy	F.	of uniform composition
___ 8.	genesis	G.	origin
___ 9.	homogeneous	H.	document wholly in the hand-
___ 10.	gene		writing of its author
___ 11.	cosmogony	I.	original model
___ 12.	gerontic	J.	creation of the universe
___ 13.	catholic	K.	universal
___ 14.	holograph	L.	insensitivity
___ 15.	eupeptic	M.	chief foe
		N.	transmitter of hereditary
			character
		O.	sensation
		P.	optimistic
		Q.	interpreting the world in terms
			of human experience

2. Indicate whether each statement is true or false by circling T
    or F.

T F   1. Proboscis, an uncomplimentary synonym for "nose,"
            etymologically means "feeder."
T F   2. Holistic means "emphasizing the organic unity of the
            whole."
T F   3. The gods of the ancient Romans and Greeks were not
            anthropomorphized.
T F   4. Ebenezer Scrooge, in Dickens' A Christmas Carol, is a
            classic example of a misanthrope.
T F   5. Primitive peoples who eat human flesh practice
            anthropophagy.
T F   6. The Greek astral and the Latinate stellar are synonyms.

T F 7. A <u>blimpologist</u> specializes in treating the grossly
          overweight.
T F 8. Words like "moo" and "bleat" are <u>onomatopoeic</u>.
T F 9. <u>Pediatricians</u> specialize in treating disorders of the
          feet.
T F 10. The <u>aster</u> derives its name from its star-shaped
          flowers.

3. Words of Interest. Supply the appropriate word from the list
    below.

	<u>Word</u>	<u>Etymological Meaning</u>	<u>Current Meaning</u>
1.	_____	lover of mankind	humanitarian
2.	_____	star sailor	person trained for space flight
3.	_____	something old-fashioned	use of an outmoded expression or style
4.	_____	perceiver	a person who is highly sensitive to the beautiful
5.	_____	unfavorable aspect of a star	calamity
6.	_____	chief builder	a person who designs buildings
7.	_____	pertaining to poor digestion	gloomy; irritable
8.	_____	burned whole	devastation, esp. by fire
9.	_____	little star	a star (*) used as a reference mark
10.	_____	mind doctor	M.D. who specializes in mental disorders

aesthete	asterisk	dyspeptic
archaism	astronaut	holocaust
architect	athlete	philanthropist
archives	disaster	psychiatrist

4. **Review**: Supply the missing prefix or base.

1. belief in no gods   a _ _ _ ism

2. mercy death   eu _ _ _ _ _ _ ia

3. a second marriage   di _ _ _ y

4. occurring at the same time   _ _ _ chronous

5. formless   _ morphous

6. empty tomb   ceno _ _ _ _

7. excessive growth   _ _ _ _ _ trophy

8. a singing back: recantation   palin _ _ e

9. booklover   _ _ _ _ _ ophile

10. affecting all people   pan _ _ _ ic

11. loss of memory   a _ _ _ sia

12. self-centered   ego _ _ _ _ _ ic

13. having a secret name   _ _ _ _ _ onymous

14. devilish   dia _ _ _ ical

15. to transform   _ _ _ _ morphose

16. story of a person's life   _ _ ography

17. place-name   top _ _ _ _

18. foot doctor   pod _ _ _ _ ist

19. hater of mankind   mis _ _ _ _ _ _ e

20. pertaining to good
    digestion   eu _ _ _ _ ic

5. **Review:** Supply the appropriate word from the list below.

WHICH SPECIALIST ARE YOU LIKELY TO CONSULT . . .

1. if you have skin problems?   _____

2. if you are interested in the
   aspect and influence of the
   stars on your future?   _____

3. if you are troubled concerning
   matters of the soul?   _____

4. if you are interested in the
   origin and development of
   your own species?   _____

5. if you need your corns removed?   _____

6. if you are experiencing problems
   associated with old age?   _____

7. if you find an Indian burial
   mound on your property?   _____

8. if you need advice on the care
   and feeding of your honey bees?   _____

9. if you discover natural gas on
   your property?   _____

10. if you are designing your own
    home?   _____

11. if you are tracing your family's
    pedigree?   _____

12. if you want your pet parrot (who
    now is deceased) preserved by
    having it stuffed and mounted?   _____

13. if you want to buy a rare book? _____

14. if you need to know the true
    meaning of a word? _____

15. if your children's teeth need
    straightening? _____

anthropologist dermatologist gerontologist
archaeologist   entomologist orthodontist
architect   etymologist   podiatrist
astrologer   genealogist   taxidermist
bibliopole   geologist   theologian

6. **Optional Latin Review:** Verbs of Destruction. Match each word
   with the base(s) from which it derives.

___ 1.	eradicate	A. CAPIT-, (CIPIT-)
___ 2.	destroy	B. CED-, CESS-
___ 3.	decimate	C. CUMB-, CUB-
___ 4.	annihilate	D. DECI(M)-
___ 5.	purge	E. FAC-, (FIC-), FACT-, (FECT-)
___ 6.	exterminate	F. I-, IT-
___ 7.	nullify	G. MOV-, MOT-
___ 8.	dissolve	H. NIHIL-
___ 9.	amputate	I. NUL(L)-
___ 10.	disintegrate	J. PUNG-, PUNCT-
___ 11.	perish	K. PURG-
___ 12.	sacrifice	L. PUT-
___ 13.	expunge	M. RADIC-
___ 14.	disassemble	N. RAP-, RAPT-, (REPT-)
___ 15.	decapitate	O. SACR-, (SECR-)
___ 16.	rape	P. SIMIL-, SIMUL-
___ 17.	expire	Q. SOLV-, SOLUT-
___ 18.	succumb	R. SPIR-
___ 19.	cease	S. STRU-, STRUCT-
___ 20.	remove	T. TANG-, (TING-), TACT-
		U. TERMIN-

7. **Optional Greek Review:** Select the appropriate mythological figure(s) from the list below.

1. Sylvan deity with cloven hoof _____

2. Visage that launched a thousand ships _____

3. Ruler of the gods renowned for philandering _____

4. Aliferous steed _____

5. A hero of the Trojan War with a bad case of homesickness _____

6. Hero who performed twelve difficult feats _____

7. Goddess born by cephalectomy _____

8. Hippanthropic creatures _____

9. One look is all it took to be immarbleized _____

10. Canine guard of the gates of hell _____

11. Woman virulently opposed to her ex-husband's remarriage _____

12. Hero with a vulnerable sole _____

Achilles	Helen	Odysseus
Athena	Hercules	Pan
Centaurs	Medea	Pegasus
Cerberus	Medusa	Zeus

LESSON VIII

1. CHROM(AT)-; CRI-; ETHN-; PHA(N)-

   Match each word with the best definition.

___	1. chromatic	A.	a review
___	2. criterion	B.	relating to races
___	3. critique	C.	to express forcefully
___	4. oneirocritic	D.	pertaining to color
___	5. ethnology	E.	cultural anthropology
___	6. ethnic	F.	a standard
___	7. theophany	G.	an observable circumstance
___	8. emphasize	H.	transparent
___	9. diaphanous	I.	visible appearance of a deity
___	10. phenomenon	J.	dream interpreter

2. PHIL-; PHON-; POLY-; THERM-

   Match each word with the best definition.

___	1. megaphone	A.	booklet
___	2. stereophonic	B.	caused by heat
___	3. symphonic	C.	belief in many gods
___	4. polygon	D.	instrument that measures temperature
___	5. polygyny	E.	concordant
___	6. polytheism	F.	state of having more than one wife at the same time
___	7. philter	G.	love potion
___	8. pamphlet	H.	a many-sided figure
___	9. thermometer	I.	producing the effect of three-dimensional sound
___	10. thermal	J.	a cone-shaped instrument that magnifies the voice

3. Words of Interest. Supply the appropriate word from the list below.

	Word	Etymological Meaning	Current Meaning
1.	_____	stage actor	dissembler
2.	_____	fig-shower	servile flatterer
3.	_____	decision	a decisive or crucial moment
4.	_____	the saying of the same things	needless repetition
5.	_____	(literary) selection	a pastoral poem
6.	_____	a sound in response	a song of praise or gladness; hymn
7.	_____	appearance	imagination; daydream
8.	_____	an instrument that records many things	lie detector
9.	_____	lover of lights	matchbook collector
10.	_____	a gathering up	miscellanea of selected literary passages

analects	fantasy	polygraph
anthem	hypocrite	polyptych
crisis	philately	sycophant
eclogue	phillumenist	tautology

4. Indicate whether each statement is true or false by circling T or F.

T F 1. Philogyny is not a prerequisite for a philanderer.
T F 2. Philippa (PHIL- + [H]IPP-) is an appropriate name for an equestrienne.
T F 3. Phony derives from the Greek base PHON-.

T F 4. The word <u>polymath</u> refers to an exceptionally gifted
           mathematician.
T F 5. A person suffering from <u>achromatopsia</u> is color-blind.
T F 6. <u>Philately</u> is an example of an avocation.
T F 7. <u>Phantasmagoria</u> may refer to a scene composed of many
           images.
T F 8. <u>Criticaster</u> is another name for a movie reviewer on
           radio or television.
T F 9. <u>Ciao</u> is an Italian loan word.
T F 10. Americans who travel in Europe and assume that everyone
           speaks English reveal their <u>ethnocentricity</u>.
T F 11. A <u>lexicographer</u> is a writer of a dictionary.
T F 12. <u>Diacritical</u> marks facilitate pronunciation by
           "distinguishing between" sounds.
T F 13. A <u>polydipsiac</u> is a person with excessive thirst.
T F 14. <u>Canopy</u> belongs to the CANON- family of words.
T F 15. Someone who is <u>ectomorphic</u> may be urged by a physician
           to go on a reducing diet.

5. **Review:** Words with Religious Associations. Match each word
    with the base from which it derives.

___ 1.	apostle	A.	ANGEL-
___ 2.	evangelist	B.	BALL-, BOL-, BLE-
___ 3.	apocrypha	C.	BIBLI-
___ 4.	Bible	D.	CANON-
___ 5.	epiphany	E.	CRYPT-, CRYPH-
___ 6.	holocaust	F.	CYCL-
___ 7.	agnostic	G.	D(A)EMON-
___ 8.	parable	H.	DOX-, DOG-
___ 9.	canons	I.	GNO(S)-
___10.	encyclical	J.	HOL-
___11.	psalmody	K.	HOM(E)-
___12.	orthodox	L.	OD-
___13.	demonic	M.	OD-, HOD-
___14.	exodus	N.	PHA(N)-
___15.	homily	O.	STOL-, STAL-, STLE-

6. **Optional Latin Review:** Food and Drink. Match each word with the base(s) from which it derives.

___	1.	minestrone	A. AC(U)-, ACR-, ACET-
___	2.	cabbage	B. AM-
___	3.	preserves	C. BENE-, BON-
___	4.	parfait	D. CAPIT-, (CIPIT-)
___	5.	pomegranate	E. CORD-
___	6.	passion fruit	F. DIC-, DICT-
___	7.	fondue	G. FAC-, (FIC-), FACT-, (FECT-)
___	8.	purée	H. FLOR-
___	9.	horseradish	I. FUND-, FUS-, [FOUND-]
___	10.	appetizer	J. GRAN-
___	11.	cordial	K. LAT-
___	12.	flour	L. MINOR-, MINUS-, MINUT-
___	13.	port	M. PATI-, PASS-
___	14.	torte	N. PET-
___	15.	vinaigrette	O. PORT-
___	16.	viands	P. PURG-
___ ___	17.	Benedictine	Q. RADIC-
___	18.	collation	R. SERV-
___	19.	Amaretto	S. ST(A)-, STIT-, SIST-
___	20.	restaurant	T. TORT-
			U. VIV-

LESSON IX

1. Words of Interest. Supply the appropriate word from the list
   below.

Word	Etymological Meaning	Current Meaning
1. _____	a slave who led a child to and from school	teacher
2. _____	well-rounded or general education	a work covering all branches of knowledge
3. _____	generalship	military tactics
4. _____	correct writing	spelling
5. _____	person who works with the hands	a physician who treats diseases by operation
6. _____	divination by studying the hands	palmistry
7. _____	a seeing together	a condensed statement; a short summary
8. _____	a looking with one's own eyes	postmortem examination
9. _____	new (element)	a gaseous element used for illuminating signs
10. _____	of another land	foreign
11. _____	citizenship	a particular system of government
12. _____	a little something in the hand	handbook

autopsy	heterochthonous	police
calligraphy	neon	polity
chiromancy	orthography	strategy
enchiridion	pedagogue	surgeon
encyclopedia	pederast	synopsis

2.   Indicate whether each statement is true or false by circling T
     or F.

T   F   1.   The etymological meaning of <u>cosmetics</u> is "substances
              intended to bring order."
T   F   2.   A person suffering from <u>pedantry</u> should consult a
              <u>podiatrist</u>.
T   F   3.   A <u>heterodoxical</u> view is in accordance with standard
              doctrines.
T   F   4.   <u>Chiropody</u> and <u>podiatry</u> are antonyms.
T   F   5.   <u>Neologism</u> refers to the use or coinage of new words.
T   F   6.   The prehistoric <u>mastodon</u> derives its name from the
              breast-shaped projections on its molars.
T   F   7.   The etymology of <u>enthusiastic</u> is "having a god within."
T   F   8.   Cologne, Germany, derives its name from <u>Colonia
              Agrippina</u>, an early Roman colony.
T   F   9.   <u>Nevada</u> ultimately derives from the Latin for "salty";
              the state owes its name to its capital city.
T   F   10.   Sir Walter Raleigh named one of the thirteen colonies
              <u>Virginia</u> because it was "unspoiled land."

3.   <u>POL-, POLIS-</u>

     Match each word with the best definition.

____   1.   acropolis   A.   city-state
____   2.   Annapolis   B.   miniature city
____   3.   cosmopolis   C.   large city
____   4.   metropolis   D.   "new city"
____   5.   Tripoli   E.   the fortified upper part of
____   6.   necropolis   an ancient Greek city
____   7.   polis   F.   Queen Anne's city
____   8.   Naples   G.   ghost town
                               H.   "city of the dead"
                               I.   city of worldwide importance
                               J.   "triple city"

4.   **Optional Latin and Greek Review:** Place-Names. From your knowledge of Latin and Greek elements, match each toponym with its <u>etymological</u> meaning.

___	1. chersonese	A.	clear water
___	2. Florence	B.	new Scotland
___	3. Eau Claire	C.	brotherly love
___	4. Vera Cruz	D.	dry island
___	5. Thermopylae	E.	prosperous
___	6. Nova Scotia	F.	encircling
___	7. Tierra del Fuego	G.	true cross
___	8. Corpus Christi	H.	warm gates
___	9. Philadelphia	I.	body of Christ
___	10. Cyclades	J.	land of fire

5. **Review:** Circle the letter of the best definition.

1.   <u>thermal</u>: (A) a vacuum bottle (B) pertaining to heat
     (C) having to do with long underwear

2.   <u>phonetic</u>: (A) frenzied (B) serving to amplify sound
     (C) pertaining to speech sounds

3.   <u>philately</u>: (A) generosity (B) a series of love affairs
     (C) stamp collecting

4.   <u>tautology</u>: (A) needless repetition (B) entirety
     (C) study of similar expression

5.   <u>phantasmagoria</u>: (A) a series of constantly shifting
     scenes (B) spiritualism (C) extraordinarily good fortune

6.   <u>lexicon</u>: (A) a book of laws (B) dictionary (C) a
     flexible plastic

7.   <u>chromosome</u>: (A) pigment-producing cell (B) a colorful
     body (C) one of the bodies in a cell nucleus that carries
     genetic material

8.   <u>criticaster</u>: (A) a television movie reviewer (B) one who
     finds fault (C) an inferior critic

9.   <u>ethnology</u>: (A) study of animal behavior (B) cultural
     anthropology (C) study of moral values

10. pepsin: (A) an enzyme secreted by the stomach (B) a cure for indigestion (C) a soft drink

11. holistic: (A) sacred (B) emphasizing the organic unity of the whole (C) having a depression or concavity

12. epigone: (A) an angled figure (B) an inferior imitator (C) embodiment

13. astrolabe: (A) an instrument used by the ancient Greeks to determine the position of stars (B) stargazer (C) the degree of brightness of a star

14. archangel: (A) eldest angel (B) chief angel (C) youngest angel

15. embolism: (A) destructive metabolism (B) occlusion of a blood vessel (C) physiological processes of an organism

16. aesthete: (A) competitor (B) person of the highest class (C) one who affects sensitivity to the beautiful

17. syntax: (A) an additional tax (B) strategy (C) grammar

18. amorphous: (A) loving (B) lacking definite form (C) shapely

19. anomaly: (A) an assumed name (B) a marine animal with tentacles (C) abnormality

20. prognosis: (A) determination of the identity of an illness (B) forecast (C) predestination

LESSON X

1. Circle the prefixes and bases and then give the meaning of each element.

MEANINGS OF PREFIXES, BASES

1. amnesia _____

2. cacophony _____

3. cosmopolite _____

4. enthusiast _____

5. iconoclast _____

6. neologism _____

7. neophyte _____

8. optician _____

9. orthodontist _____

10. prophet _____
    (See Lesson XI)

2. PATH-

Match each word with the best definition.

____ 1. antipathy   A. poignancy
____ 2. pathological   B. lack of feeling
____ 3. empathy   C. aversion
____ 4. pathos   D. compassionate
____ 5. sympathetic   E. caused by disease
____ 6. apathy   F. ascribing of feelings to objects;
                               vicarious experiencing of the
                               feelings of others

3. Words of Interest. Supply the appropriate word from the list below.

	Word	Etymological Meaning	Current Meaning
1.	_____	forgetful and lazy	sluggish
2.	_____	work	unit of work (in physics)
3.	_____	treasure	dictionary of synonyms and antonyms
4.	_____	something put in be-side something else	pair of signs ( ) used to indicate an aside
5.	_____	a thing devoted (to evil)	a curse; object of loathing
6.	_____	storehouse	pharmacy
7.	_____	something burned in	fluid used for writing
8.	_____	perception from afar	extrasensory communication
9.	_____	the act of speaking otherwise	symbolic narrative
10.	_____	burning heat (of midday)	tranquillity; serenity
11.	_____	bad character	mania
12.	_____	a standing out from oneself; derangement	rapture
13.	_____	an unpublished story	telling of a short, amusing incident
14.	_____	to brand	to burn with fire for curative purposes
15.	_____	something given against	medicine to counteract the effects of poison

allegory	calm	hypothesis
anathema	cauterize	ink
anecdote	dynamite	lethargic
antidote	dynasty	parenthesis
apothecary	ecstasy	telepathy
cacoëthes	erg	thesaurus

4. ALL-; CAC-; CAU(S)-; DO-; DYN(AM)-; ERG-, URG-; PHY-; PHYSI-;
STA-; THE-

Match each word with the best definition.

____ 1. parallel
____ 2. cacology
____ 3. caustic
____ 4. holocaust
____ 5. dose
____ 6. dynasty
____ 7. dynamo
____ 8. liturgy
____ 9. physique
____10. metaphysical
____11. stadium
____12. apostate
____13. hypothetical
____14. antithesis
____15. thesis

A. a body of rites
B. corrosive; biting
C. measured quantity of a drug
D. sports arena
E. body build
F. a powerful family
G. opposition
H. complete destruction
I. a proposal set forth for consideration
J. deserter of a cause or religion
K. producing an effect
L. conjectural
M. mispronunciation
N. analogous
O. calisthenics
P. an energetic person
Q. supernatural; abstruse

5. Indicate whether each statement is true or false by circling T or F.

T F 1. Dossier ultimately derives from the Greek base DO-.
T F 2. The name Theodore means "gift of God."
T F 3. "May he/she rest in peace" is an epithet once commonly inscribed on tombs.
T F 4. Cacography can refer to incorrect spelling or illegible handwriting.
T F 5. A red-letter day originally signified a holy day.

T F   6. Medical examiners are specialists in pathology.
T F   7. The frequently heard pronunciation of "athlete" as
           three syllables (ath-a-lete) illustrates the linguistic
           phenomenon of epenthesis.
T F   8. Cranioclast is another term for barroom "bouncer."
T F   9. The ancient Druids practiced dendrolatry.
T F 10. The word doll probably originated as a nickname for
           "Dorothy."

6. For further practice using familiar and unfamiliar Greek
    bases, supply the appropriate word from the list below.

    PHIL-

    1. a connoisseur of wine   _____

    2. affection for mankind   _____

    3. thriving in strong light   _____

    4. a lover of France or the
        French   _____

    5. a lover of learning and
        literature   _____

    6. a bacterium that grows best
        in warm temperatures   _____

    7. having an affinity for
        animals   _____

    8. fond of music   _____

    9. a friend or supporter of
        the Greeks   _____

    10. a booklover   _____

    11. a tree-loving plant   _____

    12. a connoisseur of high-
        fidelity sound reproduction   _____

    13. having a strong affinity
        for water   _____

14. a tendency to bleed pro-
    fusely   _____

15. a lover of England or the
    English   _____

Anglophile   philanthropy
audiophile   philharmonic
bibliophile   philhellene
Francophile   philodendron (XXV)
hemophilia   philologist
hydrophilic (XIII)   photophilous (XIV)
oenophile   thermophile
philanderer (XI)   zoophilous (XIII)

LAT(E)R-

Worship of . . .

1. idols   _____

2. work   _____

3. books   _____

4. evil spirits   _____

5. icons   _____

6. fire   _____

7. the dead   _____

8. the sun   _____

9. animals   _____

10. a deity   _____

bibliolatry   heliolatry (XII)
demonolatry   necrolatry (XII)
ergolatry   pyrolatry
iconolatry   theolatry
idolatry   zoolatry (XIII)

Part II, Lesson X

7.   **Review:** Supply the appropriate synonym from the list below.

1.   myth   _____

2.   mimic   _____

3.   apotheosis   _____

4.   comedian   _____

5.   enchiridion   _____

6.   dialogue   _____

7.   chaos   _____

8.   neophyte   _____

9.   diaphanous   _____

10.   antagonist   _____

11.   anathema   _____

12.   endogenous   _____

13.   analogous   _____

14.   epistle   _____

15.   cosmos   _____

adversary	imitate	native
confusion	legend	novice
conversation	malediction	similar
deification	manual	transparent
humorist	missive	universe

LESSON XI

1. KINE-, CINE-; GYN(E)-, GYN(A)EC-; LITH-, LITE-; MIS-; PHE(M)-,
    PHA-; SCHIZ-, SCHIS-; STERE-; TYP-

    Match each word with the best definition.

    ___ 1. kinetic
    ___ 2. cineast
    ___ 3. psychokinesis
    ___ 4. misogynist
    ___ 5. monolith
    ___ 6. lithography
    ___ 7. blame (n.)
    ___ 8. aphasia
    ___ 9. blaspheme
    ___10. prophet
    ___11. euphemism
    ___12. schism
    ___13. stereophonic
    ___14. archetype
    ___15. atypical

    A. loss of speech
    B. division
    C. woman hater
    D. caused by motion
    E. a single, massive block
        of stone
    F. picture tube
    G. culpability
    H. unusual
    I. devotee of movies
    J. producing a three-dimensional
        effect of sound
    K. to revile
    L. lumber
    M. original model
    N. a printing process using
        flat stones or metal plates
    O. mind controlling matter
    P. substitution of an innocuous
        expression for an offensive
        one
    Q. person who speaks for God

2. Indicate whether each statement is true or false by circling T
    or F.

    T F 1. Idiot originally referred to a private person who chose
              to refrain from public office.
    T F 2. The term hermaphrodite derives from Hermaphroditus, the
              androgynous offspring of Hermes and Aphrodite.
    T F 3. A man who suffers from gynephobia is likely to be a
              philanderer.
    T F 4. The etymological meaning of idiosyncrasy is "one's own
              private mixture."
    T F 5. Originally a gossip was a godparent.
    T F 6. The Greek phatic and the Latinate fatidic are synonyms.
    T F 7. A misologist dislikes discord of any kind.

T F   8. Men who put women on lofty pedestals might be described as <u>gyneolatrous</u>.
T F   9. Originally a <u>bonfire</u> was for burning bones.
T F 10. <u>Chartreuse</u> is the name of a color, a yellow-green liqueur, and a monastery near Grenoble, France.
T F 11. People who say that certain activities are "women's work" or "men's work" are perpetuating a <u>stereotype</u>.
T F 12. If someone has ingested poison, an <u>anecdote</u> must be administered immediately.
T F 13. <u>Boutique</u> and <u>apothecary</u> belong to the same family of words.
T F 14. <u>Orgy</u> ultimately derives from the Greek base GE-.
T F 15. <u>Apothegm</u> and <u>aphorism</u> are opposite in meaning.

3. Review: Supply the appropriate synonym from the list below.

1. dynast   _____

2. synopsis   _____

3. prophecy   _____

4. metathesis   _____

5. cinema   _____

6. demos   _____

7. prolepsis   _____

8. symphonic   _____

9. hypothesis   _____

10. eclectic   _____

11. prognosticative _____

12. sympathy   _____

13. antithetical   _____

14. polychromatic   _____

15. lexicon   _____

Part II, Lesson XI

anticipation   movies   prediction
compassion   multicolored   prescient
consonant   opposite   selective
conspectus   populace   supposition
dictionary   potentate   transposition

4. Review: Circle the bases in the following words and then
    match each with the best definition.

___ 1. cosmopolite   A. empty tomb

___ 2. epiphany   B. conforming to usual beliefs

___ 3. cenotaph   C. a combining into a single entity

___ 4. mimesis   D. comprehensive presentation

___ 5. Thanatos   E. to execrate

___ 6. chronometer   F. visible appearance of a deity

___ 7. panorama   G. a newborn child

___ 8. homotaxis   H. death personified in Greek myth

___ 9. antagonize   I. inability to read

___10. synthesis   J. a "world citizen"

___11. orthodox   K. to provoke hostility

___12. peripheral   L. imitation

___13. anathematize   M. marginal

___14. neonate   N. a very accurate timepiece

___15. alexia   O. similarity in arrangement

5. **Optional Latin Review:** Words with Religious Associations. Match each word with the base from which it derives.

___	1. commandments	A.	CANT-, (CENT-), [CHANT-]
___	2. reparation	B.	FA(B)-, FAT-, FESS-, FAM-
___	3. chant	C.	GRAD-, GRESS-
___	4. congregation	D.	GRAT-
___	5. service	E.	GREG-
___	6. transgress	F.	MAN(U)-
___	7. convert	G.	NOMEN-, NOMIN-
___	8. grace	H.	NON-
___	9. Vulgate	I.	PAR-
___	10. unitarian	J.	REG-, (RIG-), RECT-
___	11. noon	K.	SERV-
___	12. rector	L.	SCRIB-, SCRIPT-
___	13. confessional	M.	UN-
___	14. denominational	N.	VERT-, VERS-
___	15. scripture	O.	VULG-

6. **Optional Latin Review:** Match each word with its <u>etymological</u> meaning.

___	1. sonnet	A.	to return to one's fatherland
___	2. biceps	B.	sated
___	3. sad	C.	war-waging
___	4. cull	D.	removal of meat
___	5. evolve	E.	new growth
___	6. enchant	F.	to unfold
___	7. repair	G.	two-headed
___	8. haughty	H.	runner
___	9. frail	I.	to cast a spell on
___	10. belligerent	J.	breakable
___	11. foreclose	K.	to gather
___	12. recruit	L.	to shut outside
___	13. carnival	M.	one who cannot speak
___	14. corsair	N.	little song
___	15. infant	O.	high; lofty

REVIEW OF LESSONS VII-XI

1. Match each word with the best definition.

```
____  1. genethliac          A. redundant
____  2. phantom             B. vigorous; energetic
____  3. doxology            C. concerned with the whole
____  4. tautologous            instead of the parts
____  5. overdose            D. causing disease
____  6. allegorical         E. ghost
____  7. pathogenic          F. to take an excessive amount
____  8. acrolith               of a drug
____  9. holistic            G. statue with extremities
____ 10. dynamic                of stone
                             H. figurative
                             I. hymn of praise
                             J. pertaining to birthdays
```

2. Supply the missing prefix or base to form the **antonym** of each word.

```
    1. hyperesthesis        _ _ _ _ esthesia

    2. homogeneous          _ _ _ _ _ ogeneous

    3. eupeptic             _ _ _ peptic

    4. misanthrope          _ _ _ _ anthropist

    5. monogamy             _ _ _ _ gamy

    6. heterodox            _ _ _ _ odox

    7. antipathy            _ _ _ pathy

    8. polygyny             poly _ _ _ _ y

    9. euphony              _ _ _ ophony

   10. prologue             _ _ _ logue
```

3. Circle the prefixes (if any) and bases in the following words
    and give the meaning of each element. Then indicate whether
    each word is a noun or an adjective by circling N or A.

		PREFIX	BASE(S)		
1.	phonetics	_____	_____	N	A
2.	geriatric	_____	_____	N	A
3.	technical	_____	_____	N	A
4.	hyperkinesis	_____	_____	N	A
5.	neophyte	_____	_____	N	A
6.	misogynist	_____	_____	N	A
7.	hypocrisy	_____	_____	N	A
8.	optician	_____	_____	N	A
9.	cosmopolite	_____	_____	N	A
10.	emblematic	_____	_____	N	A
11.	prognosis	_____	_____	N	A
12.	anathema	_____	_____	N	A
13.	aesthete	_____	_____	N	A
14.	astral	_____	_____	N	A
15.	euphemism	_____	_____	N	A
16.	schizogenic	_____	_____	N	A
17.	exodontia	_____	_____	N	A
18.	apostate	_____	_____	N	A
19.	emphatic	_____	_____	N	A
20.	dynast	_____	_____	N	A

Part II, Review VII-XI

4. Match each word with the best definition.

____ 1. synergy	A.	lacking color
____ 2. stereotyped	B.	worship of images
____ 3. idiocy	C.	pertaining to a particular culture
____ 4. achromatic	D.	opposing religion
____ 5. pedagogy	E.	sarcastic
____ 6. caustic	F.	relating to medicine
____ 7. antithetical	G.	art of teaching
____ 8. iatric	H.	teamwork
____ 9. iconolatry	I.	expensive
____10. ethnic	J.	extreme stupidity
	K.	contrasting
	L.	conventional

5. Indicate whether each statement is true or false by circling T or F.

T F 1. The word <u>pamphlet</u> originally referred to a humorous, amatory work of the 12th century.

T F 2. <u>Cincinnati</u> is named after the famous Roman general Cincinnatus.

T F 3. The etymology of <u>Gallipoli</u> is "city of the Gauls."

T F 4. The English <u>good-bye</u> is a contraction of "God be with you."

T F 5. <u>Parliament</u> belongs to the BALL-, BOL-, BLE- family of words.

T F 6. In the expression "to eat humble pie," <u>humble</u> owes its spelling to folk etymology.

T F 7. "A stitch in time saves nine" is an example of an <u>apothegm</u>.

T F 8. The word <u>talent</u> originally referred to an amount of money.

T F 9. The expression "flash in the pan" derives from the California gold rush of 1849.

T F 10. The etymology of <u>chiropractor</u> is "one who works with the feet."

LESSON XII

1. Words of Interest. Supply the appropriate word from the list below.

    1. study of ancient writing   _____

    2. self-taught   _____

    3. gourmet   _____

    4. physician who treats the
        mind   _____

    5. self-rule   _____

    6. brightly colored   _____

    7. elaborate cemetery of an
        ancient city   _____

    8. palmistry   _____

    9. "The Unrelenting One": the
        Greek Fate who cut the
        thread of life   _____

    10. erotic interest in corpses   _____

    11. a pastoral composition   _____

    12. "household management":
        frugality in expenditure   _____

    13. a world in miniature   _____

    14. a person sensitive to super-
        natural forces; a medium   _____

    15. prophetic   _____

Atropos	gastronome	necropolis
autodidactic	idyll	paleography
autonomy	mantic	psychedelic
chiromancy	microcosm	psychiatrist
economics	necrophilia	psychic

2. AUT-; GASTR-; HELI-; IDE-; MICR-; NECR-; PAL(A)E-; PSEUD-;
    PSYCH-; TROP-

    Match each word with the best definition.

____	1. automatic	A. soul or mind
____	2. gastric	B. plant that turns toward the sun
____	3. apotropaic	C. mechanical
____	4. idea	D. pertaining to primitive man
____	5. microscopic	E. very small
____	6. necrophagous	F. gourmet
____	7. paleanthropic	G. false; counterfeit
____	8. pseudo	H. pertaining to the stomach
____	9. psyche	I. the act of nurturing by the sun
____	10. heliotrope	J. notion
		K. feeding on carrion
		L. intended to ward off evil

3. Indicate whether each statement is true or false by circling T
    or F.

T F   1. A person suffering from necrophobia is unlikely to
           pursue a career as a mortician.
T F   2. Sunflowers belong to the genus Helianthus.
T F   3. During the summer months, beaches are filled with
           present-day heliolaters.
T F   4. The word authentic derives from the Greek bases AUT- +
           THE-.
T F   5. Agricultural students take courses in agronomy.
T F   6. Necrology and obituary do not mean the same thing.
T F   7. A person who needs a dream interpreted should consult
           an oneiromancer.
T F   8. Micropaleontology is the study of large fossils.
T F   9. Australian aborigines are autochthonous peoples.
T F   10. The word idolater, besides referring to a worshiper of
           idols, can pertain to someone who admires an object too
           intensely.
T F   11. Etymologically, inaugurate means "to consult the omens"
           before engaging in an important matter.
T F   12. Pseudonym and nom de plume are both synonyms for "pen
           name."
T F   13. The etymology of neophyte is "new growth."
T F   14. An expression that is parenthetical "adds something
           beside."

T F 15. Little Rock, Arkansas, was formerly known as "Last Chance Gulch."

4. Supply the appropriate word from the list below.

IF YOU LIVE IN A(N) . . .

1. _____, the majority rule.

2. _____, the mob rules.

3. _____, all rule equally.

4. _____, the best people rule.

5. _____, those divinely guided rule.

6. _____, two regents rule.

7. _____, a few, usually for corrupt and selfish purposes, rule.

8. _____, the old rule.

9. _____, women rule.

10. _____, a single regent rules.

11. _____, the father rules.

12. _____, technical experts rule.

13. _____, there is an absence of government.

14. _____, the rich rule.

15. _____, the military rule.

anarchy	gynecocracy	patriarchy
aristocracy	monarchy	plutocracy
democracy	ochlocracy	stratocracy
dyarchy	oligarchy	technocracy
gerontocracy	pantisocracy	theocracy

5. Supply the missing base.

    1.   study of life   _ _ ology

    2.   study of humankind   _ _ _ _ _ _ _ ology

    3.   study of the earth   _ _ ology

    4.   study of God   _ _ _ ology

    5.   study of the elderly   _ _ _ _ _ _ ology

    6.   study of the mind   _ _ _ _ _ ology

    7.   study of the blood   _ _ _ _ _ ology

    8.   study of family trees   _ _ _ _ alogy

    9.   study of evil spirits   _ _ _ _ _ ology

  10.   study of form and structure   _ _ _ _ _ ology

  11.   study of insects   en _ _ _ ology

  12.   science that deals
        with the skin   _ _ _ _ _ _ ology

  13.   science that deals with
        the universe   _ _ _ _ ology

  14.   divination of the supposed
        influence of the stars   _ _ _ _ ology

  15.   study of cultures   _ _ _ _ ology

6.   Review: Supply the missing base.

1.   pertaining to color   c _ _ _ _ _ _ ic

2.   lover of mankind   _ _ _ _ anthropist

3.   world citizen   cosmo _ _ _ ite

4.   having many forms   _ _ _ _ morphous

5.   unit of work   e _ _

6.   little star (*)   _ _ _ _ _ isk

7.   one who speaks
     for God   pro _ _ _ t

8.   original model   arche _ _ _ e

9.   relating to three-
     dimensional sound   _ _ _ _ _ ophonic

10. the movies   _ _ _ _ ma

7.   Optional Latin Review: Words with Religious Associations.   Match each word with the base(s) from which it derives.

___ 1.	deity	A.	ANIM-
___ 2.	animism	B.	CARN-
___ 3.	oracle	C.	CRUC-
___ 4.	genius	D.	DE-, DIV-
___ 5.	immortals	E.	FAC-, (FIC-), FACT-, (FECT-)
___ 6.	crucify	F.	FER-
___ 7.	invocation	G.	GEN-
___ 8.	prayer	H.	MIGR-
___ 9.	portent	I.	MORT-
___ 10.	auspices	J.	OR-
___ 11.	sacrifice	K.	PLIC-, PLEX-
___ 12.	transmigration	L.	PREC-
___ 13.	supplication	M.	SACR-, (SECR-)
___ 14.	reincarnation	N.	SPEC-, (SPIC-), SPECT-
___ 15.	offering	O.	TEND-, TENT-, TENS-
		P.	VOC-, VOK-

8. **Review:** Personal Names. Match each name with its
    <u>etymological</u> meaning.

____	1. Adelphe (cf. Philadelphia)	A.	defender of men
____	2. Cosmo	B.	of the resurrection
____	3. Evangeline	C.	bearer of victory
____	4. Georgette	D.	good news
____	5. Isidora	E.	dear to God
____	6. Christopher	F.	lover of horses
____	7. Theophila	G.	gift of Isis
____	8. Alexander	H.	sister
____	9. Jason (IATR-)	I.	of the holy name
____	10. Jerome (= Hieronymus)	J.	order
____	11. Nicodemus	K.	well-born
____	12. Philippa	L.	Christ-bearer
____	13. Berenice	M.	victory over the people
____	14. Eugene	N.	healer
____	15. Anastasia	O.	little farmer

9. **Optional Latin Review:** Personal Names. Match each name with the
    base from which it derives.

____	1. Dominic	A.	AM-
____	2. Vera	B.	DE-, DIV-
____	3. Justin	C.	DOM(IN)-
____	4. Lucius	D.	FID-
____	5. Vivian	E.	GRAT-
____	6. Faith	F.	JUR-, JUST-
____	7. Valerie	G.	LUC-
____	8. Grace	H.	NASC-, NAT-
____	9. Diana	I.	PATR-, PATERN-
____	10. Victor	J.	ST(A)-, STIT-, SIST-
____	11. Natalie	K.	VAL-
____	12. Patrick	L.	VER-
____	13. Amanda	M.	VID-, VIS-
____	14. Constance	N.	VINC-, VICT-
____	15. Prudence	O.	VIV-

NOTE: Students may wish to use library resources to determine the
etymological meanings of their first <u>and</u> last names.

LESSON XIII

1. <u>ACR-; HIER-; HYDR-; MEGA(L)-; OLIG-; PATR-; PATRI-; SOPH-;
   TELE-; XEN-; ZO-</u>

   Match each word with the best definition.

   ____ 1. acrostic
   ____ 2. hieratic
   ____ 3. dehydrated
   ____ 4. megalomaniac
   ____ 5. megalopolis
   ____ 6. oligopoly
   ____ 7. patriarch
   ____ 8. patriot
   ____ 9. sophist
   ____ 10. sophomore
   ____ 11. telekinetic
   ____ 12. telepathy
   ____ 13. xenophobia
   ____ 14. xenogamy
   ____ 15. zoophagous

   A. a market condition of few sellers
   B. "wise fool"
   C. priestly
   D. fear of foreigners or strangers
   E. producing motion in objects
      without physical means
   F. deprived of water
   G. carnivorous
   H. Patrick Henry, for example
   I. populated area embracing several
      metropolises
   J. composition in verse, in which
      the first letters of each line
      form a word or phrase
   K. cross-fertilization
   L. person suffering from delusions
      of grandeur
   M. mental communication
   N. male leader of a clan or family
   O. person skilled in fallacious
      reasoning

2. Indicate whether each statement is true or false by circling T
   or F.

   T F 1. An <u>acrophobic</u> is unlikely to pursue a career as an
            <u>acrobat</u>.
   T F 2. Etymologically, a <u>prophet</u> speaks for God.
   T F 3. <u>Hydrophobia</u> is another name for rabies.
   T F 4. The etymology of <u>Vermont</u> is "purple mountain."
   T F 5. People who are careless or clumsy often suffer from
            <u>dropsy</u>.
   T F 6. Etymologically, <u>zodiac</u> refers to the imaginary band of
            animals that encircles the heavens.
   T F 7. The term <u>hieroglyphics</u>, which once referred exclusively
            to the sacred writing of the ancient Egyptians, can now
            pertain to illegible handwriting.

T F   8. <u>Patristic</u> and <u>paternal</u> mean the same thing.
T F   9. The word <u>audiophile</u> is an example of a hybrid (Latin AUD- + Greek PHIL-).
T F 10. Animal crackers are <u>zoomorphic</u>.

3. For further practice with Greek bases, supply the appropriate answer from the lists below.

MANIAS: <u>An obsession with</u> . . .

1. bibliomania   _____

2. choreomania   _____

3. cynomania   _____

4. dipsomania   _____

5. entomomania   _____

6. gynemania   _____

7. kleptomania   _____

8. monomania   _____

9. pyromania   _____

10. zoomania   _____

animals	dogs	one thing
birds	drinking	running
books	fire	stealing
dancing	insects	women

PHOBIAS: <u>An irrational fear of</u> . . .

1. agoraphobia   _____

2. algophobia   _____

3. androphobia   _____

4. claustrophobia   _____

5. gamophobia   _____

6. kinesophobia   _____

7. necrophobia   _____

8. neophobia   _____

9. pyrophobia   _____

10. taphephobia   _____

11. thanatophobia   _____

12. toxicophobia   _____

13. triskaidekaphobia   _____

animals	fire	new things
being buried	marriage	open spaces
alive	men	pain
dead bodies	movement	poison
death	narrow spaces	thirteen

The possibilities for manias and phobias are endless. There is
even a maniaphobia (fear of insanity). Using your knowledge of
Greek bases, construct others that describe yourself, friends,
or relatives. Be as fanciful as you wish.

Part II, Lesson XIII

4. Review: Match each word with the best definition.

____ 1. pedant
____ 2. architrave
____ 3. beta
____ 4. microbe
____ 5. chromatics
____ 6. energetic
____ 7. glossary
____ 8. optical
____ 9. carbohydrate
____ 10. system
____ 11. dialect
____ 12. apologize
____ 13. pancreas
____ 14. police
____ 15. sophism

A. any of a group of chemical
    compounds that constitute a
    major animal food group
B. organization
C. false argument
D. gland that secretes digestive
    enzymes
E. the second brightest star of
    a constellation
F. a regional variety of language;
    jargon
G. minute life form that causes
    disease
H. a collection of terms in a
    special field
I. a force that maintains order
J. to express regret for an error
K. the science of color
L. pertaining to the eye
M. vigorous
N. a molded band around a rectan-
    gular opening
O. person who makes an ostentatious
    show of learning

LESSON XIV

1. <u>-METER, -METRY; -SCOPE</u>

   Supply the appropriate word **from the list below.**

   1. a line of poetry with six
      metrical feet   _____

   2. an optical instrument that
      produces a variety of pat-
      terns using bits of colored
      glass   _____

   3. an instrument for viewing
      distant objects   _____

   4. an instrument for measuring
      atmospheric pressure   _____

   5. an instrument for marking
      exact time in music   _____

   6. an instrument for viewing
      small objects   _____

   7. perfect proportion   _____

   8. an optical instrument for
      viewing objects in an other-
      wise obstructed field of
      vision   _____

   9. a spiritual overseer   _____

   10. circumference of a two-
       dimensional figure   _____

   barometer   meter   periscope
   bishop   metronome   symmetry
   hexameter   microscope   taximeter
   kaleidoscope   perimeter   telescope

2. Words of Interest. Supply the appropriate word from the list below.

	Word	Etymological Meaning	Current Meaning
1.	_____	beautiful voice	keyboard musical instrument with steam whistles
2.	_____	deep sound	a male voice between tenor and bass
3.	_____	large world	the universe as a whole
4.	_____	having equal legs	having two equal sides
5.	_____	the rock	a masculine first name
6.	_____	long (mark)	a horizontal line placed over a vowel to show that it has a long sound
7.	_____	beautiful strength	gymnastic exercises
8.	_____	rock oil	a fossil fuel
9.	_____	view in every direction	a continuous unfolding of events
10.	_____	no place	a place of ideal perfection
11.	_____	beautiful handwriting	elegant penmanship
12.	_____	light-writing	process of producing images on sensitized surfaces by the action of light
13.	_____	celery rock	herb used as garnish
14.	_____	writings	writing found on walls
15.	_____	occult learning	alluring attractiveness

baritone	graffiti	parsley
calisthenics	isosceles	Peter
calligraphy	macron	petroleum
calliope	macrocosm	photography
glamour	panorama	utopia

3. -GRAM, -GRAPH

Match each word with the best definition.

___	1.	autobiography	A.	penmanship
___	2.	graphic	B.	illegal gain
___	3.	graphite	C.	a short, often satirical poem
___	4.	graft	D.	a person's own life story
___	5.	grammar	E.	inadvertent repetition of letters or words in copying
___	6.	epigram	F.	a word formed by transposing the letters of another
___	7.	program		
___	8.	anagram	G.	a plan or schedule
___	9.	chirography	H.	inscription
___	10.	dittography	I.	lifelike
			J.	study of the inflection and syntax of a language
			K.	soft carbon used in pencils

4. Indicate whether each statement is true or false by circling T or F.

T F 1. An archaeologist is more likely than most people to encounter petroglyphs.

T F 2. Etymologically, the verb arrive means "to reach shore."

T F 3. Engrave ultimately derives from the Greek combining form -GRAPH.

T F 4. A photosensitive person is camera-shy.

T F 5. Bandy, as in the expression "to bandy words," derives from the game of tennis.

T F 6. The word juggernaut (Hindi Jagannath) has come to mean any large, powerful force that crushes anything in its path.

T F 7. John D. Rockefeller was a great lycanthropist.

T F 8. Checkmate, which derives from Persian, etymologically means "the king is dead."

Part II, Lesson XIV

T F 9. The expression <u>salad days</u> refers to youthful inexperience, the time of life when people are still "green."
T F 10. An <u>isobar</u> is a line on a weather map that connects points of equal pressure.

5. **Review:** Words with Religious Associations. Match each word with the best definition.

____ 1. neophyte
____ 2. anathema
____ 3. anthem
____ 4. apotheosize
____ 5. apostate
____ 6. blasphemy
____ 7. catholic
____ 8. cenobite
____ 9. crypt
____10. dogma
____11. epistle
____12. liturgy
____13. synod
____14. prophet
____15. allegory

A. church council
B. universal
C. expression of human experience by symbolic figures
D. an underground burial chamber
E. rites for public worship
F. to deify
G. a new convert
H. one of the letters in the New Testament
I. sacrilege
J. Moses, for example
K. hymn or song of praise
L. doctrine
M. curse; denunciation
N. person who abandons a previous loyalty or religious faith
O. member of a religious community

6. **Optional Latin Review:** Match each Latin word or phrase with the best definition.

____ 1. facsimile
____ 2. memorandum
____ 3. animus
____ 4. fiat
____ 5. cui bono
____ 6. per diem
____ 7. magnum opus
____ 8. pro tempore
____ 9. ad nauseam
____10. cum laude

A. greatest work of an artist
B. authorization
C. "to whose advantage"
D. to a sickening degree
E. for the time being
F. hostility
G. for ten cents only
H. with academic distinction
I. a written reminder
J. for each day
K. reproduction
L. truce

254

LESSON XV

1. GON-; LAB-, LEP-, LEM-; MES-; PHRA-; STROPH-

    Match each word with the best definition.

____	1. polygon	A.	disorder of the central nervous system marked by convulsions
____	2. syllable	B.	inverted word order
____	3. narcoleptic	C.	smallest unit of speech
____	4. epilepsy	D.	transitional period of the Stone Age
____	5. lemma	E.	many-sided figure
____	6. mesencephalon	F.	circumlocution
____	7. Mesolithic	G.	theme or subject
____	8. Mesopotamia	H.	ancient land between two rivers
____	9. paraphrase	I.	to restate the context of a passage in a new form
____	10. periphrasis	J.	punctuation mark (') indicating omission of letters
____	11. antiphrasis	K.	midbrain
____	12. apostrophe	L.	use of a word in a sense opposite to its generally accepted meaning
____	13. catastrophe	M.	experiencing frequent, uncontrollable attacks of sleep
____	14. strophe	N.	stanza
____	15. anastrophe	O.	disaster

2. Review: Match each item with the appropriate description.

____	1. medical examiner	A.	a misanthrope
____	2. "swift-footed" Achilles	B.	an avocation
____	3. Scrooge	C.	an epithet
____	4. Mormons	D.	an epitaph
____	5. Jackson	E.	a pseudonym
____	6. turtle	F.	former polygynists
____	7. philately	G.	person who conducts autopsies
____	8. New Zealand	H.	the antipodes of England
____	9. Here Lies Penelope Potts	I.	an amphibian
____	10. Lewis Carroll	J.	a patronymic

3. **Optional Latin Review:** Travel. Match each word with the base(s) from which it derives.

___	1. suitcase	A.	AG-, (IG-), ACT-
___	2. compartment	B.	AQU(A)-
___	3. train	C.	BI-, BIN-
___	4. agent	D.	CRUC-
___	5. bicycle	E.	CUR(R)-, CURS-
___	6. stagecoach	F.	[JOURN-]
___	7. automobile	G.	I-, IT-
___	8. aquaplane	H.	JAC-, JECT-
___	9. voyage	I.	LOC-
___	10. journey	J.	MOV-, MOT-
___	11. cruise	K.	MUT-
___	12. bus	L.	OMN-
___ ___	13. locomotive	M.	PART-
___	14. reservation	N.	PED-
___	15. jet	O.	PORT-
___	16. expedition	P.	SEQU-, SECUT-
___	17. itinerary	Q.	SERV-
___	18. excursion	R.	ST(A)-, STIT-, SIST-
___	19. commuter	S.	TRACT-
___	20. transportation	T.	VI(A)-

4. **Optional Latin and Greek Review:** Animals. Match each word with its _etymological_ meaning.

___	1. dinosaur	A.	flame
___	2. mastiff	B.	earth dog
___	3. terrier	C.	river horse
___	4. mastodon	D.	leaper
___	5. flamingo	E.	clear singer
___	6. canary	F.	thick skin
___	7. hippopotamus	G.	fear-inspiring lizard
___	8. dromedary	H.	bone crusher
___	9. rhinoceros	I.	horned nose
___	10. chanticleer	J.	flat foot
___	11. salmon	K.	accustomed to the hand
___	12. osprey	L.	bird from the "dog islands"
___	13. platypus	M.	runner
___	14. pachyderm	N.	shadow tail
___	15. squirrel	O.	nipple-shaped tooth

LESSON XVI

1. Match each word with the best definition.

___	1. monocle	A.	double vision
___	2. hemiplegia	B.	a copying machine
___	3. diplopia	C.	having five digits
___	4. tripod	D.	an eyeglass for one eye
___	5. pentadactyl	E.	a verse of seven feet
___	6. heptameter	F.	having eight parts
___	7. hectograph	G.	a group of four
___	8. octamerous	H.	to assume total control of something
___	9. monopolize	I.	three-legged stand
___	10. tetrad	J.	paralysis of one side of the body

2. Indicate whether each statement is true or false by circling T or F.

T F 1. Vampires are believed to practice hematophagy.

T F 2. Hex ("to bewitch") ultimately derives from the Greek numerical base HEX(A)-.

T F 3. The etymological meaning of pagan is "infidel."

T F 4. The word chiliad ("one thousand") is a synonym for "millennium."

T F 5. An ancient Roman would have been unfamiliar with the gesture "thumbs down."

T F 6. The Decalogue is a drama both famous and unique in antiquity for its ten speaking parts.

T F 7. Attic originally meant "pertaining to Attica" (the region in which Athens is located).

T F 8. Gymnosophists ("naked philosophers") were ascetic wise men of ancient India who wore little or no clothing.

T F 9. By extension, the word octopus can describe any person or organization with wide-reaching control.

T F 10. Miniature is related to the Latin base MINOR-, MINUS-, MINUT-.

3. Words of Interest. Supply the appropriate word from the list
   below.

	Word	Etymological Meaning	Current Meaning
1.	_____	ten thousand	a large, indefinite number
2.	_____	three folds	set of three hinged panels
3.	_____	situation in which one is seized in two directions	difficult situation
4.	_____	first gluing	diplomatic etiquette
5.	_____	one letter	two or more initials combined into one character
6.	_____	ten contests	contest composed of ten athletic events
7.	_____	every seven days	weekly
8.	_____	place of solitude	place occupied by a religious order
9.	_____	second actor	person who acts as a foil to another
10.	_____	first model	a model on which something is patterned
11.	_____	something with five corners	a five-pointed, star-shaped figure
12.	_____	100 oxen	sacrifice of 100 oxen; any great slaughter
13.	_____	square	tile used in mosaics; token
14.	_____	twofold sheet	document of an educational degree
15.	_____	little table	horizontal bar for acrobatic exercises

decathlon	hecatomb	pentacle
deuteragonist	hyphen	protocol
dichotomy	kilowatt	prototype
dilemma	monastery	tessera
diploma	monogram	trapeze
hebdomadal	myriad	triptych

4. **Review:** Supply the appropriate base(s) or combining form from which the following words derive.

1. enthusiasm _____

2. grotto _____

3. amnesty _____

4. boutique _____

5. philter _____

6. ink _____

7. surgery _____

8. ballet _____

9. fancy _____

10. bishop _____

11. glamour _____

12. idiom _____

13. palsy _____

14. blame _____

15. monk _____

16. anthem _____

BALL-, BOL-, BLE-
CAU(S)-
CH(E)IR-
CRYPT-, CRYPH-
ERG-, URG-
-GRAPH, -GRAM
IDI-
LY-
MNE-

MON-
PHA(N)-
PHE(M)-, PHA-
PHIL-
PHON-
-SCOPE
THE- ("god")
THE- ("to place")

5. **Optional Latin Review:** Supply the missing letters to form an Anglo-Saxon equivalent of each Latinate word.

    1. premonition   fore _ _ _ _ ing

    2. altitude   h _ _ _ _ _

    3. innate   in _ _ _ _

    4. regal   k _ _ _ ly

    5. flex   b _ _ _

    6. immortal   d _ _ _ _ less

    7. gratitude   t _ _ _ _ fulness

    8. oration   s _ _ _ _ _

    9. manual   _ _ _ _ book

  10. decapitate   be _ _ _ _

6. **Optional Latin and Greek Review:** Plants. Match each word with its _etymological_ meaning.

___ 1.	aster		A.	gold flower
___ 2.	gladiolus		B.	a flower that never grows old
___ 3.	cyclamen		C.	tree-loving
___ 4.	rhododendron		D.	of the liver (three-lobed plant)
___ 5.	nasturtium		E.	water cup
___ 6.	ageratum		F.	pensive
___ 7.	pansy		G.	circle
___ 8.	heliotrope		H.	flesh-colored flower
___ 9.	philodendron		I.	star
___ 10.	hydrangea		J.	turning with the sun
___ 11.	eglantine		K.	nose twister
___ 12.	chrysanthemum		L.	little sword
___ 13.	carnation		M.	prickly
___ 14.	hepatica		N.	lily flower
___ 15.	fleur-de-lis		O.	rose tree

LESSONS XVII, XVIII, & XIX

1. Match each word with the best definition.

___ 1. choreographer	A. "islands of dark-skinned people"
___ 2. glyph	B. pedagogy
___ 3. Polynesia	C. relating to navigation or ships
___ 4. Melanesia	D. itinerant
___ 5. Eros	E. composer of dances
___ 6. nautical	F. "group of many islands"
___ 7. aeronautics	G. political dominance of one nation
___ 8. plethora	H. person who practices extreme
___ 9. bucolic	self-discipline
___10. didactics	I. a carving in relief
___11. hedonic	J. characterized by pleasure
___12. paroxysm	K. superfluity
___13. hegemony	L. sudden, violent emotion
___14. peripatetic	M. pastoral
___15. ascetic	N. god of love
	O. art of flight

2. Use a check to indicate whether the following words are
    singular or plural.

	SINGULAR	PLURAL
1. analysis	___	___
2. criteria	___	___
3. dilemma	___	___
4. epitome	___	___
5. hoi polloi	___	___
6. kudos	___	___
7. metamorphoses	___	___
8. odea	___	___
9. phenomenon	___	___
10. thesauri	___	___

3. Words of Interest. Supply the appropriate word from the list below.

	Word	Etymological Meaning	Current Meaning
1.	_____	seasickness	queasiness
2.	_____	dog's tail	attention getter
3.	_____	a wound	psychic disorder caused by injury
4.	_____	hostile speech	controversial argument
5.	_____	stain; pollution	noxious or foreboding atmosphere
6.	_____	turning like oxen in plowing	alternate lines written from left to right and from right to left
7.	_____	riddle	something difficult to understand
8.	_____	depth	anticlimax; sentimentalism
9.	_____	fixed point	memorable date; extended period of time
10.	_____	hunger of an ox	eating disorder characterized by constant hunger
11.	_____	flood	violent upheaval
12.	_____	gigantic statue	amphitheater
13.	_____	mixing bowl	hole; depression in the earth
14.	_____	brand; tattoo	mark of shame
15.	_____	excessiveness	redundancy

Part II, Lessons XVII, XVIII, & XIX

bathos	crater	nausea
boustrophedon	cynosure	pleonasm
bulimia	enigma	polemic
cataclysm	epoch	stigma
colosseum	miasma	trauma

4. Indicate whether each statement is true or false by circling T or F.

T F 1. Sardine and sardonic belong to the same Greek family of words

T F 2. Etymologically, the word belfry has nothing to do with bells or bell towers.

T F 3. In ancient Rome, as in our own times, loud clapping signified enthusiastic acclamation of a theatrical performance.

T F 4. Etymologically, expeculation and cattle rustling are synonyms.

T F 5. Originally shambles referred to the devastation after an earthquake.

T F 6. Siderodromophobia means "morbid fear of unidentified flying objects."

T F 7. Swan song acquires its present meaning from the once held notion that swans, sensing the approach of death, burst into melodious song.

T F 8. The word bikini is onomatopoeic.

T F 9. There are some loan words, such as hors d'oeuvre, that never completely become English.

T F 10. The word scene originally referred to a tent used by Greek actors as a dressing room.

5. **Review:** Choose the correct answer by circling A or B.

1. identification of
   a disease: (A) prognosis   (B) diagnosis

2. humorous story: (A) anecdote   (B) antidote

3. hag: (A) crony   (B) crone

4. married to two
   individuals
   simultaneously: (A) bigamous   (B) digamous

263

Part II, Lessons XVII, XVIII, & XIX

5. formal debate: (A) parlance   (B) parry

6. nutritional: (A) tropic   (B) trophic

7. shapeless: (A) amorphous   (B) amorous

8. person sensitive
    to the beautiful: (A) aesthete   (B) athlete

9. theatrical perfor-
    mance: (A) hysterics   (B) histrionics

10. sacrifice of many
    victims: (A) hector   (B) hecatomb

11. concert hall: (A) odeum   (B) odium

12. biting: (A) caustic   (B) caudal

13. indifference: (A) apathy   (B) empathy

14. producing fever: (A) pyrrhic   (B) pyretic

15. inscription on a
    tomb: (A) epitaph   (B) epithet

16. science dealing with
    the eyes: (A) ophiology   (B) ophthalmology

17. to curse: (A) anesthetize   (B) anathematize

18. to predict: (A) procrastinate   (B) prognosticate

19. widespread: (A) endemic   (B) pandemic

20. emblem: (A) allegory   (B) allegiance

REVIEW OF LESSONS XII-XIX

1. Match each word with the best definition.

___ 1. metempsychosis	A. paralyzed with fear
___ 2. automatic	B. poetry composed by persons of low intelligence
___ 3. ideogram	C. group of persons organized according to rank
___ 4. petrified	D. inflammation of the stomach
___ 5. hydrophilic	E. witchcraft
___ 6. ego trip	F. a written symbol, such as "&" or "="
___ 7. acronical	G. project undertaken principally to satisfy one's self-image
___ 8. gastritis	H. transmigration
___ 9. hierarchy	I. having a strong affinity for water
___10. necromancy	J. spontaneous
	K. occurring at sunset
	L. flatulence

2. Indicate whether each statement is true or false by circling T or F.

T F 1. Explode owes its origin to the Roman theater, where the audience indicated its displeasure by "clapping the actor off the stage."

T F 2. Picky eaters might be termed oligophagous.

T F 3. The name of the flower zinnia ultimately derives from the Greek base XEN-.

T F 4. Etymologically, Mediterranean and Mesopotamia describe places situated between land or water.

T F 5. Paragon derives from the Greek base GON-.

T F 6. Octopus admits two plurals, "octopuses" and "octopi."

T F 7. The etymology of impersonate is "to put on another's mask."

T F 8. Glamour originally referred to occult learning.

T F 9. The expression "to tide us over" derives from the sport of sailboat racing.

T F 10. In classical times the word martyr meant "victim."

T F 11. Bucolic derives from the Greek for "cow."

T F 12. <u>Salary</u>, <u>sausage</u>, and <u>salad</u> all come from the Latin base for "salt."

T F 13. The Colosseum in Rome derived its name from its proximity to an enormous statue of the emperor Nero.

T F 14. The etymology of <u>brand-new</u> is "fresh from the blacksmith's fire."

T F 15. <u>Squire</u> originally referred to the shield bearer of a knight.

3. By combining Greek elements, form English words with the following meanings.

1. rule by one   _____

2. the writing of one's own life story   _____

3. worship of the dead   _____

4. a lover of the French   _____

5. fear of being buried alive   _____

6. person obsessed with himself or herself   _____

7. scientist who studies celestial phenomena   _____

8. irrational fear of women   _____

9. an instrument that can view small objects   _____

10. the study of human lives and cultures   _____

Part II, Review XII-XIX

4. Words of Interest: Supply the appropriate word from the list below.

	Word	Etymological Meaning	Current Meaning
1.	_____	solitary person	male member of a religious community
2.	_____	a turning back of the enemy	a prize for victory or achievement
3.	_____	six threads	heavy medieval silk fabric
4.	_____	small animal figure	an imaginary belt of constellations
5.	_____	a commonplace	subject; theme
6.	_____	beautiful old age	monk of the eastern church
7.	_____	hour observer	astrological pre-diction
8.	_____	taken together	unit of spoken speech
9.	_____	seasickness	loud or unpleasant sound
10.	_____	choral dance	company of singers

callipygian   monk   syllable
caloyer   noise   topic
choir   saltpeter   trophy
horoscope   samite   zodiac

5. Supply the missing prefix or base to form the <u>antonym</u> of each
    of the following words.

    1. neolithic   _ _ _ _ olithic

    2. microcephalic   _ _ _ _ cephalic

    3. cacography   _ _ _ _ igraphy

    4. perihelion   _ _ helion

    5. macrocosm   _ _ _ _ ocosm

6. Match each word with the best definition.

    ____ 1. pseudo   A. instrument that measures
    ____ 2. barometer   atmospheric pressure
    ____ 3. telegnosis   B. growing toward or away from
    ____ 4. erotica   the light
    ____ 5. diorama   C. in a drama, the final
    ____ 6. sophistry   resolution of the plot
    ____ 7. chorea   D. plausible but false reasoning
    ____ 8. catastrophe   E. a mark of punctuation (-)
    ____ 9. glyptic   F. wisdom
    ____10. phototropic   G. clairvoyance
    ____11. paraphrase   H. to reword
    ____12. isonomy   I. equality of political rights
    ____13. hyphen   J. scene reproduced in three
    ____14. encomium   dimensions
    ____15. hoi polloi   K. false; pretended
                               L. knowledge acquired through
                                   travel abroad
                               M. disease of the nervous system
                               N. a formal expression of praise
                               O. pertaining to carving
                               P. the common people
                               Q. literary or artistic works
                                   intended to arouse sexually

7. Circle the numerical base(s) in each word and then give the meanings of the bases.

1. hectograph _____

2. triad _____

3. kilogram _____

4. heptarchy _____

5. protein _____

6. pentameter _____

7. dilemma _____

8. triskaidekaphobia _____

9. dichotomize _____

10. monocle _____

GREEK REVIEW (Lessons III-XIX)

1. Match each word with the best definition.

___ 1. gastronome	A.	first martyr in any cause
___ 2. hematogenous	B.	worship of images
___ 3. thaumaturgy	C.	general
___ 4. iconolatry	D.	petrified plant
___ 5. psychiatrist	E.	gourmet
___ 6. protomartyr	F.	self-taught
___ 7. ethnocentricism	G.	instrument that indicates
___ 8. autodidactic		variations in pressure
___ 9. dendrolite	H.	physician who treats mental
___10. parallel		disorders
___11. oligarchy	I.	dentist who straightens teeth
___12. baroscope	J.	magic
___13. egomaniacal	K.	producing blood
___14. orthodontist	L.	extremely self-centered
___15. encyclical	M.	belief in the superiority of
		one's own culture
	N.	rule by the few
	O.	similar

2. Indicate whether each statement is true or false by circling T or F.

T   F   1. A cell with a "fondness for acids" creates acidophilus milk.

T   F   2. Originally subtle referred to a type of fishing gear.

T   F   3. A misandrist is the feminine counterpart of a misogynist.

T   F   4. A person who dates only foreigners may be described as a xenophile.

T   F   5. The French adieu and the Spanish adios are roughly equivalent to the English good-bye.

T   F   6. Criticaster is composed of two Greek bases, CRI- and AST(E)R-.

T   F   7. According to some etymologists, dicker derives from the Latin base DECI(M)-.

T   F   8. Ruminate originally meant "to chew the cud."

T   F   9. The word lewd has undergone degeneration of meaning; originally the word referred to "the uneducated laity."

T   F 10. George is a particularly appropriate name for a farmer.

Part II, Review

3. Words of Interest. Supply the appropriate word from the list below.

Word	Etymological Meaning	Current Meaning
1. _____	stitching of songs	musical composition of irregular form
2. _____	instrument for viewing beautiful shapes	optical instrument that produces a variety of patterns using bits of colored glass
3. _____	slanderer	Satan
4. _____	new growth	beginner
5. _____	a person's word	conditional release of a prisoner
6. _____	a private citizen	foolish person
7. _____	full armor	a complete array
8. _____	matters of arrange-ment	maneuvers for gaining success
9. _____	all imitation	the telling of a story through body movements only
10. _____	chief sea	expanse of water with scattered islands
11. _____	tube	mounted gun
12. _____	pedestal; balcony	a bench in a church

archipelago	kaleidoscope	parole
cannon	neophyte	pew
devil	panoply	rhapsody
idiot	pantomime	tactics

Part II, Review

4. Words of Interest. Supply the appropriate word from the list below.

1. Egyptian writing   _____

2. something remarkable or
    unusual   _____

3. powerful explosive used
    for blasting   _____

4. water clock   _____

5. a specialty shop   _____

6. ancient two-handled vessel   _____

7. song of praise   _____

8. model of excellence   _____

9. art of improving the
    memory   _____

10. place where official
    records are kept   _____

11. beautifying   _____

12. anticipatory   _____

amphora	clepsydra	mnemonics
anthem	cosmetic	paragon
archives	dynamite	phenomenon
boutique	hieroglyphics	proleptic

5. Match each word with the appropriate equivalent.

_____ 1. obituary   A. epistle
_____ 2. lunatic   B. mantic
_____ 3. division   C. anomalous
_____ 4. irregular   D. schism
_____ 5. transcendental E. agonizing
_____ 6. similar   F. pyretic
_____ 7. missive   G. maniac
_____ 8. divinatory   H. necrology
_____ 9. febrile   I. analogous
_____10. excruciating   J. metaphysical

6. Match each word with the appropriate equivalent.

_____ 1. caustic   A. transitory
_____ 2. peripatetic   B. resuscitation
_____ 3. trophic   C. palmistry
_____ 4. anabiosis   D. nutritive
_____ 5. chronic   E. itinerant
_____ 6. chiromancy   F. library
_____ 7. tautology   G. redunduncy
_____ 8. ephemeral   H. celestial
_____ 9. bibliotheca   I. habitual
_____10. ethereal   J. mordant

7. Circle the prefixes (if any) and bases and give the meaning of each element; then indicate whether each word is a noun, an adjective, or a verb by circling N, A, or V.

MEANINGS OF PREFIXES, BASES

1. dyslexia _____ N A V

2. aphelion _____ N A V

3. catholicism _____ N A V

4. evangelize _____ N A V

5. pedagogics _____ N A V

6. perigee _____ N A V

7. paradoxical _____ N A V

8. asterisk _____ N A V

9. stereotypic _____ N A V

10. prognosticate _____ N A V

11. epidermal _____ N A V

12. demonic _____ N A V

13. polygamous _____ N A V

14. cinema _____ N A V

15. empathy _____ N A V

16. antiphrasis _____ N A V

17. politician _____ N A V

18. anonymous _____ N A V

19. cataclysm _____ N A V

20. podium _____ N A V

Part II, Review

8. Supply the missing base.

1.	empty tomb	ceno _ _ _ _
2.	pain of longing for things past	nost _ _ _ ia
3.	having good digestion	eu _ _ _ _ ic
4.	a false or assumed name	_ _ _ _ _ onym
5.	a diacritical mark that indicates a long sound	_ _ _ _ on
6.	pertaining to sight	_ _ _ ical
7.	a mentally disturbed person with delusions of greatness	_ _ _ _ _ omaniac
8.	study of form and structure	_ _ _ _ _ ology
9.	holding a different opinion	_ _ _ _ _ odoxical
10.	composed of the same kind of parts	_ _ _ ogeneous
11.	science of colors	_ _ _ _ _ _ _ ics
12.	person who can speak three languages	tri _ _ _ _
13.	extrasensory perception	_ _ _ _ pathy
14.	world in miniature	micro _ _ _ _
15.	study of ancient writing	_ _ _ _ ography
16.	first or original model	_ _ _ _ otype
17.	contest of ten athletic events	_ _ _ athlon
18.	woman hater	_ _ _ ogynist
19.	birth of the gods	_ _ _ ogony
20.	lover of human beings	_ _ _ _ anthrope

9. Circle the bases or combining forms in the following words and then match each with the appropriate equivalent.

___ 1.	diathesis	A.	omniscient
___ 2.	apathetic	B.	amorous
___ 3.	epigraph	C.	disposition
___ 4.	nautical	D.	quadrangular
___ 5.	pansophic	E.	insectivorous
___ 6.	tetragonal	F.	bisectional
___ 7.	polyanthous	G.	inscription
___ 8.	erotic	H.	multiflorous
___ 9.	dichotomous	I.	impassive
___10.	entomophagous	J.	naval

APPENDIXES

APPENDIX A

LATIN AND GREEK EQUIVALENTS

The following list of Latin and Greek equivalents is not intended
to be exhaustive, but does contain a number of the more important
prefixes and bases introduced in English Words from Latin and
Greek Elements.

Prefixes

Latin	Greek	Meaning
ab-, a-, abs-	apo-, ap-	from; away from
ambi-	amphi-	both; around
con-, com-	syn-, sym-	with
dis-, di-	dia-, di-	asunder; apart
ex-, e-	ec-, ex-	out; out of
extra-, extro-	exo-, ecto-	outside
in-, im-	en-, em-	in; into
intra-, intro-	endo-, ento-	within
pre-/pro-	pro-	before; in front of
sub-	hypo-, hyp-	below
super-	hyper-	over

Appendix A

Bases

Latin	Greek	Meaning
AC(U)-, ACR-, ACET-	ACR-	a point
AG-, (IG-), ACT-	AGOG(UE)-	to lead
ART-	ARTHR-	art; joint
AUD-	AESTHE-, ESTHE-	to hear; to perceive
BI-, BIN-	DI-, DIPL-	two; twice
CAPIT-, (CIPIT-)	CEPHAL-	head
CENT-	HECT-	a hundred
CERN-, CRET-	CRI-	to decide; to judge
CORD-	CARDI-	heart
DECEM-; DECI(M)-	DEC(A)-	ten; tenth
DOC-, DOCT-	DOX-, DOG-	to teach; teaching
DU-	DICH-	(in) two
EGO-	EGO-	I
FA(B)-, FAT-, FESS-, FAM-	PHE(M)-, PHA-	to say
FER-	PHER-, PHOR-	to bear
FOLI-	PHYLL-	leaf
GEN-/NASC-, NAT-	GEN(E)-, GON-	to produce
GENER-, GEN-	GEN(E)-	race; kind
GNO-, NO-, NOT-	GNO(S)-	to know
GRAV-	BAR-	heavy; weight
LEG-, (LIG-), LECT-	LOG-, [LOGUE-], LECT-	to pick; to read

Appendix A

Latin	Greek	Meaning
LUC-, LUMIN-	LEUC-, LEUK-	light; white
MAGN-	MEGA(L)-	great; large
MEDI-	MES-	middle
MILL-	KILO-	a thousand
MON-	MNE-	to warn; to remember
NOC-, NOX-, NIC-, NEC-	NECR-	to kill; corpse
NOMEN-, NOMIN-	ONYM-	name
NOV-	NE-	new
NOVEM-; NON-	ENNEA-	nine; ninth
OCT-; OCTAV-	OCT(A)-	eight; eighth
PATI-, PASS-	PATH-	to feel; to suffer
PATR-, PATERN-	PATR-	father
PED-	POD-	foot
PRIM-	PROT-	first
QUINQUE-; QUINT-	PENT(A)-	five; fifth
RAP-, RAPT-, (REPT-)	LAB-, LEP-, LEM-	to seize
SCI-	SCHIZ-, SCHIS-	to know (to separate one from another)
SEMI-	HEMI-	half
SEPT(EM)-, SEPTIM-	HEPT(A)-	seven; seventh
SEX-; SEXT-	HEX(A)-	six; sixth
SIMIL-, SIMUL-	HOM(E)-	the same
SOLV-, SOLUT-	LY-	to loosen

Appendix A

Latin	Greek	Meaning
SPEC-, (SPIC-), SPECT-	-SCOPE	to see
ST(A)-, STIT-, SIST-	STA-	to stand
TEND-, TENT-, TENS-	TON(US)-	to stretch
TRI-; TERTI-	TRI-	three; third
UND-	HYDR-	wave; water
VID-, VIS-	IDE-	to see; object of vision
VIV-	BI-	to live; life

APPENDIX B

ANSWERS TO REVIEW SECTIONS

Part I: Word Elements from Latin

Review of Lessons II-VII (pp. 45-50)

1.   1--ad; 2--sub; 3--con; 4--ex; 5--dis; 6--in; 7--ad; 8--in;
     9--ob; 10--sub.

2.   1--de; 2--se; 3--ab; 4--pro; 5--ante; 6--post; 7--extro;
     8--inter; 9--ad; 10--di; 11--retro; 12--col; 13--intro;
     14--trans; 15--per; 16--super; 17--re; 18--pre; 19--in;
     20--circum.

3.   1--OPTIM; 2--GRAV; 3--SENS; 4--PEND; 5--PLEN; 6--ANIM;
     7--CANT; 8--EQU; 9--FIN; 10--CENT; 11--PRIM; 12--LOQU;
     13--UN; 14--JUR; 15--ENNI; 16--VOC; 17--ALIEN; 18--DU;
     19--MALE; 20--PART; 21--VERB; 22--MULT; 23--PED;
     24--SANCT; 25--MAGN.

4.   1--D; 2--J; 3--C; 4--G; 5--I; 6--B; 7--F; 8--H; 9--E; 10--A.

5.   1--BIN; 2--DU; 3--MILL; 4--OCT; 5--PRIM; 6--QUART; 7--QUINT;
     8--SEXT; 9--SESQUI; 10--TRI.

6.   1--ante; 2--ad + retro; 3--contra; 4--extra; 5--inter;
     6--post; 7--super; 8--ultra.

7.   1--S; 2--A; 3--S; 4--A; 5--S; 6--A; 7--S; 8--A; 9--S; 10--S;
     11--A; 12--S; 13--S; 14--A; 15--S; 16--S; 17--S; 18--S;
     19--A; 20--S.

8.   1--T; 2--N; 3--Q; 4--H; 5--E; 6--R; 7--I; 8--P; 9--O; 10--D;
     11--S; 12--J; 13--F; 14--C; 15--A; 16--G; 17--L; 18--M;
     19--B; 20--K.

Appendix B

9. 1--A; 2--B; 3--A; 4--B; 5--B; 6--B; 7--B; 8--B; 9--B;
    10--B; 11--A; 12--A; 13--A; 14--B; 15--A; 16--A; 17--A;
    18--A; 19--B; 20--B.

Review of Lessons VIII-XIV (pp. 95-98)

1. 1--T; 2--T; 3--F; 4--F; 5--T; 6--T; 7--F; 8--T; 9--T; 10--T;
    11--T; 12--T; 13--T; 14--F; 15--F.

2. 1--C; 2--E; 3--D; 4--A; 5--B.

3. 1--S; 2--S; 3--S; 4--A; 5--A; 6--A; 7--S; 8--S; 9--S; 10--S;
    11--S; 12--S; 13--S; 14--A; 15--S.

4. 1--L; 2--N; 3--K; 4--M; 5--D; 6--J; 7--F; 8--A; 9--G; 10--B;
    11--O; 12--I; 13--E; 14--H; 15--C.

5. 1--NAT; 2--CAPT; 3--DIV; 4--NOV; 5--CRED; 6--VER; 7--OR;
    8--LATER; 9--LUMIN; 10--MUT; 11--PULS; 12--(P)OSIT; 13--AM;
    14--SIMIL; 15--FA; 16--CORPOR; 17--FLAT; 18--FOLI; 19--DUR;
    20--(F)ACT.

6. 1--E, TERR; 2--L, CAS; 3--H, TRACT; 4--B, DUR; 5--M, FEDER;
    6--I, GENER; 7--C, MOD; 8--F, TENU; 9--O, AQUA; 10--N, FALL;
    11--J, PAR; 12--D, TEND; 13--K, NOX; 14--G, FID; 15--A, NEC.

Review of Lessons XV-XIX (pp. 131-134)

1. 1--T; 2--T; 3--T; 4--T; 5--T; 6--T; 7--F; 8--F; 9--F; 10--T;
    11--T; 12--T; 13--T; 14--T; 15--F.

2. 1--F; 2--L; 3--K; 4--H; 5--G; 6--B; 7--I; 8--C; 9--E; 10--J;
    11--D; 12--A.

3. 1--S; 2--A; 3--S; 4--A; 5--A; 6--S; 7--S; 8--S; 9--S; 10--S;
    11--S; 12--S; 13--A; 14--A; 15--A.

4. 1--SCRIPT; 2--VIV; 3--LEG; 4--NOMIN; 5--DICT; 6--VAL;
    7--SCI; 8--FRANG; 9--SON; 10--(S)CRIB; 11--(M)INUT;
    12--CRES; 13--SOL; 14--PATRI; 15--MON.

5. 1--com + MISS + ary; 2--con + SON + ance; 3--ex + (S)ECUT +
    rix; 4--con + VAL + escence; 5--CLAM + or; 6--ac + CRET +
    ion; 7--in + QUIR + y; 8--AG + ility; 9--GRAN + ule; 10--VIV
    + acity; 11--PATRI + mony; 12--SCRIPT + orium; 13--MON +
    itor; 14--con + JECT + ure; 15--SEG + ment; 16--MINUS + cule;
    17--ACT + uary; 18--com + PASS + ion; 19--ef + FERV +
    escence; 20--FRACT + ure.

Review of Lessons XX-XXV (pp. 167-171)

1. 1--advertisement; 2--automobile; 3--blitzkrieg;
    4--memorandum; 5--disport; 6--distillery.

2. 1--B; 2--B; 3--C; 4--B; 5--A; 6--C; 7--C; 8--A.

3. 1--corrigenda; 2--nostrum; 3--agenda; 4--pace; 5--imprimatur;
    6--via; 7--memento; 8--genus; 9--animus; 10--minutiae;
    11--succubus; 12--decorum; 13--finis; 14--facsimile;
    15--credo.

4. 1--F; 2--F; 3--F; 4--T; 5--T; 6--T; 7--T; 8--F; 9--F; 10--T;
    11--T; 12--T; 13--F; 14--T; 15--T.

5. 1--A and B; 2--C; 3--B; 4--A and C; 5--B and C.

6. 1--K; 2--H; 3--E; 4--M; 5--A; 6--G; 7--Q; 8--L; 9--B; 10--O;
    11--N; 12--F; 13--D; 14--I; 15--P.

7. 1--MORT; 2--AUD; 3--GRAT; 4--PET; 5--RADIC; 6--CORD; 7--LOC;
    8--MEDI; 9--MANU; 10--CAPIT; 11--(F)LEX; 12--SPIR; 13--ALT;
    14--GNO; 15--MEDI.

8. 1--C; 2--G; 3--M; 4--D; 5--N; 6--I; 7--O; 8--A; 9--E; 10--B;
    11--F; 12--J; 13--H; 14--L; 15--K.

9. 1--J; 2--G; 3--D; 4--A; 5--F; 6--I; 7--B; 8--H; 9--C; 10--E.

Latin Review (Lessons II-XXV) (pp. 173-180)

1. 1--F; 2--T; 3--F; 4--T; 5--T; 6--T; 7--F; 8--F; 9--T; 10--T;
    11--F; 12--F; 13--T; 14--T; 15--T.

2. 1--VIS; 2--AL; 3--TERR; 4--MANU; 5--PATRI; 6--MUT; 7--SCRIB;
    8--MULT; 9--CARN; 10--MILL; 11--AUD; 12--LOC; 13--FIN;
    14--DICT; 15--AM; 16--LINE; 17--PUG; 18--MALE; 19--COG;
    20--MOV.

3. 1--con; 2--de; 3--post; 4--dis; 5--suf; 6--con; 7--pro;
    8--ex; 9--op; 10--e.

4. 1--C; 2--A; 3--B; 4--C; 5--B; 6--B; 7--A; 8--C; 9--B; 10--A;
    11--A; 12--B; 13--C; 14--A; 15--B; 16--A; 17--C; 18--B;
    19--C; 20--A; 21--B; 22--A; 23--C; 24--B; 25--A.

5. 1--B; 2--D; 3--J; 4--A; 5--I; 6--C; 7--M; 8--O; 9--E; 10--K;
    11--F; 12--N; 13--H; 14--G; 15--L.

6. 1 and 4; 3; 1, 3, and 4; 2 and 4.

7. 1--L; 2--C; 3--A; 4--H; 5--B; 6--F; 7--O; 8--N; 9--J; 10--E;
    11--M; 12--D; 13--I; 14--G; 15--K.

8. 1--L; 2--E; 3--J; 4--I; 5--H; 6--M; 7--A; 8--O; 9--F; 10--N;
    11--D; 12--K; 13--C; 14--B; 15--G.

9. 1--S; 2--S; 3--S; 4--A; 5--A; 6--A; 7--A; 8--A; 9--S; 10--A;
    11--S; 12--S; 13--S; 14--S; 15--S; 16--S; 17--A; 18--S;
    19--A; 20--S.

10. 1, 3, and 4; 1; 1, 3, and 4.

11. 1--ab + UND, A; 2--a + PART, N; 3--AQUA, N; 4--circum + FER,
    N; 5--cor + RIG, N; 6--de + FAM, N; 7--ef + FERV, V; 8--en +
    DUR, N; 9--ex + (S)ECUT, N; 10--extra + SENS, A; 11--im +
    MIGR, V; 12--LAT, N; 13--LECT, N; 14--per + TIN, A; 15--pre +
    CURS, N; 16--RAP, A; 17--SAL, A; 18--super + FLU, N;
    19--TURB, A; 20--VER, V.

*   *   *

Part II: Word Elements from Greek

Review of Lessons I-VI (pp. 209-212)

1. 1--synonym; 2--ectoderm; 3--euphoria; 4--hypotrophy;
    5--endomorph; 6--eulogistic; 7--hyperglycemia; 8--cathode;
    9--dystrophy; 10--anabasis.

2. 1--A; 2--A; 3--S; 4--A; 5--S; 6--A; 7--A; 8--A; 9--S; 10--S;
    11--S; 12--S; 13--S; 14--A; 15--S.

3. 1--podagra; 2--amnesty; 3--nostalgia; 4--pandemonium;
    5--apocrypha; 6--palinode; 7--hyperbole; 8--panacea;
    9--tome; 10--paraphernalia; 11--iconoclast; 12--canister;
    13--enthusiasm; 14--tragedy; 15--democracy.

4. 1--D; 2--A; 3--E; 4--H; 5--G; 6--B.

5. 1--F; 2--F; 3--F; 4--T; 5--F; 6--F; 7--T; 8--F; 9--T; 10--T.

6. 1--F, PAN; 2--P, STOL; 3--J, CRYPT, ONYM; 4--A, BIBLI; 5--D,
    GNOS; 6--Q, PYR; 7--C, LY; 8--M, TAPH; 9--G, CYCL; 10--B,
    LOGUE; 11--O, GLOSS; 12--E, MIM; 13--N, TROPH; 14--L, BI;
    15--H, POD.

Review of Lessons VII-XI (pp. 237-239)

1. 1--J; 2--E; 3--I; 4--A; 5--F; 6--H; 7--D; 8--G; 9--C; 10--B.

Appendix B

2. 1--hypo; 2--HETER; 3--dys; 4--PHIL; 5--POLY; 6--ORTH; 7--sym;
    8--ANDR; 9--CAC; 10--epi.

3. 1--PHON, N; 2--GER, IATR, A; 3--TECHN, A; 4--hyper, KINE, N;
    5--NE, PHY, N; 6--MIS, GYN, N; 7--hypo, CRI, N; 8--OPT, N;
    9--COSM, POL, N; 10--em, BLE, A; 11--pro, GNOS, N; 12--ana,
    THE, N; 13--AESTHE, N; 14--ASTR, A; 15--eu, PHEM, N;
    16--SCHIZ, GEN, A; 17--ex, ODONT, N; 18--apo, STA, N;
    19--em, PHA, A; 20--DYN, N.

4. 1--H; 2--L; 3--J; 4--A; 5--G; 6--E; 7--K; 8--F; 9--B; 10--C.

5. 1--T; 2--T; 3--F; 4--T; 5--T; 6--T; 7--T; 8--T; 9--F; 10--F.

Review of Lessons XII-XIX (pp. 265-269)

1. 1--H; 2--J; 3--F; 4--A; 5--I; 6--G; 7--K; 8--D; 9--C; 10--E.

2. 1--T; 2--T; 3--F; 4--T; 5--F; 6--T; 7--T; 8--T; 9--F; 10--F;
    11--T; 12--T; 13--T; 14--T; 15--T.

3. 1--monarchy; 2--autobiography; 3--necrolatry; 4--Francophile;
    5--taphephobia; 6--egomaniac; 7--astronomer; 8--gynephobia;
    9--microscope; 10--anthropology.

4. 1--monk; 2--trophy; 3--samite; 4--zodiac; 5--topic;
    6--caloyer; 7--horoscope; 8--syllable; 9--noise; 10--choir.

5. 1--PALE; 2--MEGA; 3--CALL; 4--ap; 5--MICR.

6. 1--K; 2--A; 3--G; 4--Q; 5--J; 6--D; 7--M; 8--C; 9--O; 10--B;
    11--H; 12--I; 13--E; 14--N; 15--P.

7. 1--HECT; 2--TRI; 3--KILO; 4--HEPT; 5--PROT; 6--PENTA; 7--DI;
    8--TRI[S], DEKA; 9--DICH; 10--MON.

Appendix B

Greek Review (Lessons III-XIX) (pp. 271-277)

1. 1--E; 2--K; 3--J; 4--B; 5--H; 6--A; 7--M; 8--F; 9--D; 10--O;
    11--N; 12--G; 13--L; 14--I; 15--C.

2. 1--T; 2--F; 3--T; 4--T; 5--T; 6--F; 7--T; 8--T; 9--T; 10--T.

3. 1--rhapsody; 2--kaleidoscope; 3--devil; 4--neophyte;
    5--parole; 6--idiot; 7--panoply; 8--tactics; 9--pantomime;
    10--archipelago; 11--cannon; 12--pew.

4. 1--hieroglyphics; 2--phenomenon; 3--dynamite; 4--clepsydra;
    5--boutique; 6--amphora; 7--anthem; 8--paragon; 9--mnemonics;
    10--archives; 11--cosmetic; 12--proleptic.

5. 1--H; 2--G; 3--D; 4--C; 5--J; 6--I; 7--A; 8--B; 9--F; 10--E.

6. 1--J; 2--E; 3--D; 4--B; 5--I; 6--C; 7--G; 8--A; 9--F; 10--H.

7. 1--dys, LEX, N; 2--ap, HELI, N; 3--cat, HOL, N; 4--ev,
    ANGEL, V; 5--PED, AGOG, N; 6--peri, GE, N; 7--para, DOX, A;
    8--ASTER, N; 9--STERE, TYP, A; 10--pro, GNOS, V; 11--epi,
    DERM, A; 12--DEMON, A; 13--POLY, GAM, A; 14--CINE, N;
    15--em, PATH, N; 16--anti, PHRA, N; 17--POL, N; 18--an,
    ONYM, A; 19--cata, CLYS, N; 20--POD, N.

8. 1--TAPH; 2--ALG; 3--PEPT; 4--PSEUD; 5--MACR; 6--OPT;
    7--MEGAL; 8--MORPH; 9--HETER; 10--HOM; 11--CHROMAT; 12--GLOT;
    13--TELE; 14--COSM; 15--PALE; 16--PROT; 17--DEC; 18--MIS;
    19--THE; 20--PHIL.

9. 1--C, THE; 2--I, PATH; 3--G, GRAPH; 4--J, NAUT; 5--A, PAN,
    SOPH; 6--D, TETRA, GON; 7--H, POLY; 8--B, EROT; 9--F, DICH,
    TOM; 10--E, TOM.